Creativity in primary science

2

Exploring Primary Science and Technology

Series Editor: Brian Woolnough
Department of Educational Studies, University of Oxford

Science is one of the most exciting and challenging subjects within the National Curriculum. This innovative new series is designed to help primary school teachers to cope with the curriculum demands by offering a range of stimulating and accessible texts grounded in the very best of primary practice. Each book is written by an experienced practitioner and seeks to inspire and encourage whilst at the same time acknowledging the realities of classroom life.

Current and forthcoming titles

Jenny Frost: *Creativity in primary science*
Jane Johnston: *Early explorations in science*
Anne Qualter: *Differentiated primary science*

Creativity in primary science

JENNY FROST

OPEN UNIVERSITY PRESS
Buckingham • *Philadelphia*

Open University Press
Celtic Court
22 Ballmoor
Buckingham
MK18 1XW

and
1900 Frost Road, Suite 101
Bristol, PA 19007, USA

First Published 1997

A catalogue record of this book is available from the British Library

ISBN 0 335 19552 0 (pbk)   0 335 19553 9 (hbk)

Library of Congress Cataloging-in-Publication Data

Frost, Jenny.
    Creativity in primary science / Jenny Frost.
        p.   cm. — (Exploring primary science and technology)
    Includes bibliographical references and index.
    ISBN 0–335–19552–0 (pbk) — ISBN 0–335–19553–9 (hbk)
    1. Science—Study and teaching (Elementary)—Great Britain.
I. Title. II. Series.
LB1585.5.G7F76   1996
372.3'5—dc20   96–17895
                                                        CIP

Typeset by Graphicraft Typesetters Limited, Hong Kong
Printed in Great Britain by St Edmundsbury Press,
Bury St Edmunds, Suffolk

Contents

List of figures

Series editor's preface

One of the great achievements in the educational system of England and Wales over the last decade has been the growth of science and technology teaching in the primary school. Previously this had been weak and spasmodic, often centring on the nature table and craft work; now it is well established in the curriculum of all children from the age of 5. Primary school teachers are to be congratulated on this achievement, building their science work on often uncertain foundations. This is therefore an appropriate time for this series of books which looks in detail at what has been achieved, and seeks to develop the fundamental principles that underlie the ways in which children learn and teachers teach science and technology in primary schools.

Two approaches to primary school science had been developing prior to the introduction of a National Curriculum. The first saw investigations as the focus of the children's work, studying aspects of their natural environment to develop both an insight into the underlying science and the way that scientists work. The second approach was modelled more on the way in which science had been taught in the secondary school and centred on the content of science which needed to be taught. When the National Curriculum for science was introduced in 1989 it sought, not entirely satisfactorily, to bring together these two approaches, with half the curriculum being given to explorations and investigations and half to the content of science. In this series we are seeking to explore primary science and technology further. We perceive science and technology as more than an accretion of skills and knowledge but rather as a holistic activity involving pupils' hands, minds and hearts. For the pupils to fully learn and appreciate science and technology they will need to develop their attitudes, experiences and knowledge through activities which challenge and stimulate them, and in which they find success and satisfaction. We seek both to educate children *in* science and technology and *through* science and technology, helping them both to appreciate and enjoy these subjects and through them to develop their personality and sense of self worth.

Doing science and technology is a very personal and individualistic matter. Learning science, like the learning of everything else of real worth, is a messy, unpredictable but ultimately satisfying process. One of the benefits of a National Curriculum is that it establishes the place of science and technology in the curriculum. One of the great weaknesses of the English National Curriculum is that it has prescribed the content around an assessment structure which infers linear progression foreign to the way children really learn. Children learn (differentially according to their aptitudes and strengths) by personal exploration; by testing out their ideas in discussion and writing; by being encouraged when they are on the right lines, and corrected when they seem to be heading off in the wrong direction and are using the language of science inappropriately. The teacher's vital and sensitive task is to provide the appropriate stimulation in scientific and technological contexts, to allow the children to express their thinking, and to encourage and correct them as appropriate. In such a way children will construct their own understanding and attitudes to science and technology and become members of the broader scientific and technological community.

Jenny Frost's book starts where many writers leave off, with the teachers. This is not a book about the curriculum, and how it should be taught. It is about teachers and the way that in reality, they do teach it, using their personal and creative skills and their sensitive understanding of the children to modify their teaching to meet the needs of the developing classroom situation. It focuses on, and celebrates, the ways that teachers use a wealth of experience and tacit knowledge to enrich their teaching beyond the formal demands of the curriculum. Through a series of case studies of different teachers, she illustrates ways that good classroom practice develops. She uses the analogy of a play, directed by teachers with the pupils; not a tightly scripted play, but one where improvisation occurs throughout, building on the strengths and creativity of both the teacher and the pupils to develop the story. Through personal involvement, the learning and appreciation of the subject are deeply assimilated. This book will stimulate and support teachers as they share in the creativity of others and are encouraged to build on their own personal resources in teaching and exploring primary science and technology.

Acknowledgements

I should like to thank Brian Woolnough for his invitation to write this book and for his advice during the preparation; and also Shona Mullen, the commissioning editor, for her support, guidance and constructive criticism.

I am very grateful to Siân Heaton for undertaking the task of making black and white illustrations from photographs; essential features would have been lost had we tried to use the photographs directly in the text. I also found her enthusiasm for the ideas she found in the pictures of other teachers' classrooms an endorsement of my belief that sharing the ideas was worthwhile.

Discussion with my colleagues at the Institute of Education and with the many primary teachers I have met through our courses has been invaluable over the years in fashioning my thoughts about science education in general and about primary science in particular. These have no doubt contributed to the book in many imperceptible ways.

I would like to acknowledge the following for permission to

publish material: Open University Press, the Association for Science Education, and Paul Chapman Publishers.

I have reserved until the end those to whom I owe the greatest debt, the six teachers, Anne Robertson, Esmé Glauert, Siobhan Quinlan, Claudette Bournes, Alex Lundie and Nicola Metcalf, whose teaching forms the basis of the six case studies in Chapters 3 to 8. They readily gave me permission to share their ideas with others and have patiently answered my questions. I hope that my writing does justice to their professional and intellectual expertise and generosity.

Part 1

1

Introduction – creativity in teaching

This book is about creativity in teaching, and a celebration of the skills and expertise of primary teachers in the area of science.

It stems from my involvement in the professional development of primary teachers. As science has emerged as an important part of the primary curriculum (and since 1989, as a compulsory part), so primary teachers have had to develop their professional skills and knowledge to meet the demands. Science has become an obligatory component of all initial teacher education courses. For practising teachers, school-based INSET, off-site courses and distance learning packages have been brought to bear on the subject. Publications in the field have proliferated; primary science has attracted education research from the work of the lone M.Phil/ Ph.D. student to that of large funded projects. This book examines an area which has so far had little attention, namely the ways in which primary teachers, from a whole range of different backgrounds and expertise, go about the process of planning science activities for young children.

One theme that can be found in many of the courses, publications and research projects is a 'deficit model' of primary teachers – particularly in the area of scientific knowledge. Government has funded GEST courses to enhance the scientific knowledge of teachers (Kinder and Harland 1991); research has discovered, not surprisingly, that primary teachers do not understand concepts such as energy and forces in the way a physicist would (Summers and Kruger 1992); OFSTED (1995) has reported on the lack of confidence in science particularly at the top end of Key Stage 2; teacher confidence (and particularly the lack of it) in subject-matter has been researched (Wragg *et al.* 1989) and made the focus of a recent research project in Scotland (Harlen *et al.* 1995).

While I would similarly stress the importance of subject knowledge, in the course of my work I have met a considerable number of primary teachers who claimed to have little formal knowledge of science but who created imaginative and effective learning activities for their classes. To be fair, more recent research into teacher confidence has also reported considerable increase in knowledge, attributed mainly to three or four years of implementing science in their classrooms (Carré and Carter 1993).

I began to talk increasingly with teachers about how they went about planning. This required asking them to articulate and analyse an activity which had become almost second nature to them. A variety of strategies were revealed, but also a range of stable features. They talked of thinking about the class, the individuals within it and the link between what was to be learnt and the children's previous experience and understanding. They saw themselves as the creator of events in which their classes and they could participate. They thought about their own understanding of the topic – could they put it into their own words, not just use the words in the books? They identified the significance of a fact (if a spider has eight legs – so what?). They seemed to be able to create games, problems and quizzes that involved children in using new-found ideas and hence in consolidating those ideas.

The analogy of writing a play began to emerge. The teachers seemed to be engaged in writing a play for players that they knew reasonably well, a play, however, in which everyone would improvise. The end-point was known in outline, often not just to the teacher, but to the class as well; the unfolding of the play, however, was not known. The teacher became the provider of the props, the organizer of the stage and the person who set the scene and defined roughly what was to be done; the detailed script developed as the play evolved. Teachers as co-players and producers often had to replan as they went along. I began to explore the ideas that they held in their minds which allowed the play to continue and not go completely off the rails, and yet which allowed them to change direction quite considerably from the course they had anticipated before the lesson started.

The ideas were about the nature of science; the nature of science in primary schools; the role that science plays in the education of young children; understanding children; notions of learning; knowledge of motivation; relationships between teachers and learners; relationships between teachers and science; levels of complexity of organization; awareness of resource constraints, including time; the relationships between assessment and teaching; and finally, the way in which a teacher reorganizes knowledge in the process of preparing for, and undertaking, teaching.

Chapter 2 is devoted to exploring those ideas which relate particularly to science education in primary schools. It begins with a consideration of what 'knowing some science' might entail in general, in order to give some vision of what science education in primary schools might be leading to. This is followed by a brief review of some of the research into the learning and teaching of science with young children.

The second part of the book, Chapters 3 to 8, is devoted to case studies of sequences of lessons, sometimes over periods of one or two weeks or up to a whole term. Each one is interesting in its own right and many readers may gain specific ideas for classroom teaching from the descriptions. Each example contains commentaries which relate back to the more theoretical and generalized discussions which occur in Chapter 2. They were selected as examples of good practice in science education and as exemplifying, and defining, the creativity in teaching which I had in mind.

The first case study on the teaching of a topic of parks, woods and wastelands to a mixed Years 3 and 4 class (8 to 9-year-olds) contains amongst other things the stories of Professor Sense and Professor Question, created by the teacher, Anne Robertson, to help children understand the importance of using their senses and asking questions. It shows quite clearly the ongoing link between assessment and planning throughout the topic and the careful organization of time to allow development in children of very different abilities. The teacher has a focus on learning science and is quite clear about the skills and the knowledge that she wants the class to learn. The high priority she places on children's ability to communicate is apparent. The complexity and diversity of ideas and resources which are brought together are evidence of her ability to create an imaginative experience from many different parts.

The second case study, in Chapter 4, is one which people who have been on courses at the Institute of Education are likely to have heard, because I have used it on several occasions. 'Rabbit's House' was an investigation undertaken by middle infants (Years 1 and 2, 5 to 7-year-olds) with Esmé Glauert; and it had taken something like two weeks for the whole class to finish. This was the first example where I asked a teacher to 'unpack' the planning and the organization of a teaching/learning sequence, and found that it was a far from straightforward task.

The management of time is something that features prominently in the analysis of Rabbit's House. Time is a resource that has to be divided up as part of the planning process and is one of the aspects of teaching which beginning teachers find very difficult. How do teachers plan for one afternoon, for a series of days, for this week and next? How do they help children hold their learning over long timespans?

One of the most creative aspects of this example is the ability to see the potential for a serious scientific investigation in a simple story and how to build in small but significant 'loose ends' such that children have to sort out how to do something themselves. As in many of the case studies, the teacher focuses on developing the children's ability to handle, record and interpret data; the account includes her strategies for enabling these young children to understand the significance of features of tables for recording data.

Chapter 5 contains a case study on the topic of Ourselves taught by Siobhan Quinlan, in a school in west London, just off Ladbroke Grove. It was selected initially because the classroom was like an Aladdin's cave, overflowing with interesting displays of the children's work and resource material. The class was a Year 2 class (6 to 7-year-olds) learning about skeletons and other parts of the inside of the human body. One of the key elements here was the sudden realization on the part of the children that they could do simple science investigations on themselves. Like the teacher in Rabbit's House, one of this teacher's objectives was that the children should develop their skill at recording and interpreting simple data. The personal ID cards, containing data which the children built up from their own body measurements, were carried with them to the next class to be used in a related topic a year later.

The fourth and fifth case studies, in Chapters 6 and 7, came from the Aquatech Project, which was run jointly by the Institute of Education, the London Borough of Greenwich and the Society for Underwater Technology. This project attempted to link industry with teachers and to relate school studies with the water industry. One topic is a study of the building of the Channel tunnel (Year 6) and was taught by Claudette Bournes at a school in Bexleyheath in south-east London. The other topic is related to the river Thames (Year 4, 8 to 9-year-olds) and was taught by Alex Lundie in a school in Abbey Wood, in the London Borough of Greenwich.

The Channel tunnel topic has some similarities with Rabbit's House because the explorations and investigations are relatively simple and easy to resource; but it is thinking them up in the first place which requires the inspiration. It also shows the ability of the teacher to react to an unplanned resource – the arrival of snow – to get the class to try and collect a cubic metre of snow so that they could appreciate that the tunnel boring machines were removing 1100 cubic metres of spoil per day. They never did manage to collect a cubic metre of the snow! She became aware of just how much the children had learnt from the topic the following term on the school trip to France. While there, they visited the exhibition about the tunnel, which had all the labels in French. The children were able to explain to their parents what all the pictures and diagrams were about because they understood the problems and solutions connected with building the tunnel.

The chapter on the Year 4 topic of the river Thames tracks the teacher's planning and replanning in some detail, and describes her classroom organization which allowed for children to work at their own pace. The quality of observational drawings and writing are impressive, as well as the willingness of one or two children to write about things that went wrong with their investigations as well as what went right. The sheer logistics involved – in the organization of fish and prawns from the fishmonger for close observational drawings, a paddling pool for trying out boats, a 'river' running in a plastic gutterpipe and a corner of the room devoted to a model of a yacht used for drama and role play – are significant features of this study.

The teacher in the final case study was Nicola Metcalf, teaching in a school in the London Borough of Harrow. The class is a Year 1 class (5 to 6-year-olds). She follows in detail four pairs of children as they grapple with designing investigations to find out what things people can do with and without their eyes open. She shows how it is necessary for a teacher to have sufficient insight into the thinking of these relatively young children to be able to identify what for them will be a significant investigation and discovery. Her documentation of snippets of conversation has been an invaluable resource. This particular case study was prepared initially from the teacher's own report of her research in her classroom. I have quoted extensively from it; so in this chapter more than the others the direct voice of a teacher is heard.

I believe the case studies provide good examples of the way in which teachers reorganize their knowledge of a subject in the process of teaching. The activities they create, the questions they ask, the analogies they use, the interesting stories that they tell, are all part of this reorganization. They form what Shulman (1986) called 'pedagogic content knowledge', learnt from experience, from other teachers, often fashioned in the process of teaching in response to a particular child. There is no simple way to learn them but the preconditions are teachers' own interest in, and enthusiasm and knowledge of the subject, coupled with a clear focus on the children's learning of science and a willingness to try anything to help them understand and be skilful.

The final part of the book, Chapter 9, returns to the ideas of Chapter 2 to review the six case studies and to see how they, with all the details of busy classrooms, give exemplars to illustrate the general ideas about 'knowing some science' and the processes of 'coming to know some science'.

While I was preparing this book, I was asked how I envisaged it being used and how it would be useful to both beginning teachers and practising teachers. I will venture to offer a few suggestions only.

An important function is the sharing of experience that books of this sort make possible. Teaching, like so many professions, can be isolating. After initial teacher education courses, many teachers do not have the opportunity to watch other teachers teach, although the process of appraisal is making some inroads into this isolation. To share practice, however, is not to advocate that it should be copied unquestioningly. The case studies do nevertheless translate some of the generalities and principles described in Chapters 1, 2 and 9 into specific instances, and may consequently have the function of explaining the generalities. It is the generalities that may transfer from one context to another.

The acknowledgement that teaching, and particularly the planning for teaching, is creative may be helpful, especially to beginning teachers. Each year I find that the most difficult sessions for beginning teachers are those devoted to planning. I sometimes wonder if inadvertently we have given the impression that planning is straightforward, and that there is a magic planning formula that can be applied. At the same time, the book makes clear the constraints pertaining to teaching, which mean that teachers do not have infinite choice over what they do.

The book may also be useful for those teachers who are taking an increased role in initial teacher education. As professional courses require participants to spend a larger part of their time in schools, experienced teachers will require the skill to be able to explain and discuss the craft of the classroom as well as demonstrate it.

I have had considerable encouragement from people in science teaching to write the book, to celebrate the creative aspect of teaching science. The introduction of the National Curriculum in England and Wales has increased the teaching of science in primary schools (and incidentally increased teachers' confidence to teach science (Wragg 1994)), but the attention paid to making sure all aspects are covered has taken up a lot of nervous energy and time. I realized as I was writing that the examples in the book could be analysed against the National Curriculum and they would not be found wanting. The National Curriculum in science, as such, does not prohibit creative teaching.

A comment for those readers who do not know English primary schools

I cannot be sure of the extent to which these case studies and the messages within them will translate to contexts in other countries. I believe that the more general principles concerned with learning and the ideas for simple explorations and investigations will be applicable in other places. The size of classes in the schools in this book rarely exceeds 30 children, so some of the organization may not transfer to schools where teachers are coping with much larger numbers.

An explanation also needs to be given about the apparent autonomy of teachers to select what topic they want. The National Curriculum provides outline programmes of study but allows considerable scope for the order in which topics are taught. Many schools have developed carefully planned sequences of topics to be taught throughout the school, so that the children progressively cover the requirements of the National Curriculum (DFE 1995). I have referred in several chapters to the teachers having to teach a certain topic because it was on the school's 'planning grid'. These whole-school plans generally specify the concepts in science to be taught, but not the contexts in which they are taught; consequently there is flexibility over what the teacher chooses. Teachers and schools also vary in the extent to which a topic carries the whole of the curriculum. In Chapters 3, 5 and 6, the teachers were teaching an 'integrated topic' which covered the whole of the curriculum. In the other case studies the work had a more restricted focus.

As a whole, the book should provide windows on to teaching and learning in science whatever the organization within the school.

2

Science education – aims and research

The case studies which take up two-thirds of this book focus on classroom practice and appear at first sight to be merely descriptive; they give information about the classroom, about what was taught and what was learnt, and about how it was taught and learnt. There have, however, been several influences on what has been selected and what has been emphasized, and these are explained in this chapter. One influence is my own notion of the goals of science education in general, not just in primary schools. Another influence comes from research in science education where both research questions and research findings have helped the understanding of science classrooms. Obviously the wish to use the case study material to develop the theme of creativity in teaching has influenced the way the stories have been told.

Goals of science education – 'knowing some science'

There has been, over the last two decades, a tendency to regard 'primary science' as an object separate from other learning in science, as though it has some special and different identity. I think it may at times be helpful to remove this special connotation and just think about what we mean when we say that somebody 'knows some science', and recognize that the studies undertaken in the area of science when children are in primary school form part of a learning continuum. I have therefore started by 'unpicking' this notion of 'knowing some science' by describing ten different facets of it: knowing about the natural and made world; understanding explanations; being familiar with scientific concepts; asking questions; understanding experiments; interpreting data; having technical know-how; linking science and everyday occurrences; appreciating the nature of science; appreciating the cultural significance of science.

Knowing about the natural and made worlds

To know some science is to know what can be done to objects and materials and what will happen when these things are done: for instance, that when a ball is released it falls to the ground; that when air is warmed it expands: that when a magnet is put near iron, it will attract it: that when a chicken's egg is cooked it changes, never to return to the raw state again; that when a caterpillar is fed it will grow into a moth, butterfly, or insect of some sort; that something as solid as a rock might crumble away in time . . . People who know some science will not know all the things there are to know, but will know quite a few and will be aware that there are many more that could be looked up in books, or learnt from experience or from other people.

Understanding explanation

They will also know that there are explanations of how these things happen: gravitational attraction between the ball and the earth; increased movement of molecules in heated air; alignment of the crystals in iron; irreversible chemical changes in the egg; ability of the body of a living thing to convert the food it eats into things it needs, either to fuel its body processes or to continue to build its own body; that rain and wind can slowly erode hard materials and that what was once rock may become part of the soil. They will know some of these explanations and know how they fit the phenomena. There will be many explanations that they do not know but they will be aware that these also could possibly be looked up in books.

Being familiar with scientific concepts

They may know about things like black holes, genes, electrons, atoms, molecules, galaxies, DNA, continental plates, continental drift, germs, hormones . . . and have some mental image of what they are like. They will be able to imagine sound as vibrations, light as an entity distinct from its source, electricity as a flow of electrons . . .

Asking questions

People are more inquisitive about the things they know about than about the things they do not. So people who know some science are also likely to ask questions about how things happen; what causes them to happen; what the processes involved are; how people have come to give such explanations; what evidence supports the explanations.

Understanding experiments

Experiments are taken as one of the hallmarks of science. They involve certain procedures, but in each case, experimenters have to decide how to proceed in order to extract the evidence that is needed to answer a question. People who know some science have some idea about how to design an experiment, how to collect data and possible ways of making sense of that data.

Interpreting data

People who know some science are likely not to be daunted by looking at sets of numerical data relating to the natural and material world; information on food packets; weather data; temperature and blood pressure charts at the end of a patient's bed in hospital.

This does not mean that they can interpret any set of scientific data. Understanding how data was collected and understanding the theory behind an experiment is essential for being able to interpret that data. Scientists involved in looking at the evidence from the CERN generator and interpreting it as 'nine atoms of antimatter have been produced' are unlikely to be any better than a lay person at interpreting diagnostic ultrascans in the medical field.

Having technical know-how

It is likely also that people who know some science have some technical know-how as well and could well have practical hobbies. They will be able to make some sense of technical and scientific information which is just part of everyday life. They are likely to feel at home with measuring instruments, and also with tools that require good manipulative skills, but this of course is not automatically the case.

Linking science and everyday occurrences

This may mean knowing how a thermostat works, or understanding the cycle of the sun and moon, or knowing why there is concern about deforestation and the increase of the size of the Sahara desert; or knowing where rain comes from, and really believing that all the material on this planet is being continuously recycled, even ourselves. They will not be too baffled by medical information given them in routine medical checks, nor by newspaper articles about the greenhouse effect. They may know enough about the mechanisms of genetics to know how corn seeds grow into corn and not tomatoes, and why sunflower seeds grow into sunflowers and not a rose.

Appreciating the nature of science

People who are said to know some science are also likely to have some appreciation of the nature of science, and some idea about how such knowledge and explanations have been built up and slowly accumulated over time. They will know that imagination plays a large part in science – imagining the unobservable, imagining how things might be different from common sense. They will appreciate to some extent what counts as evidence in science, and how arguments are put together. They may be aware that science experiments in a laboratory are highly controlled events and may not replicate the complex conditions that operate outside, so that inferences from the former have to be made tentatively when trying to illuminate the latter. They are also likely to recognize that knowing about what the natural world does can be very different from knowing how what it does can be explained. Teachers in particular tend to appreciate this; they have far more trouble trying to teach about electric current and voltage than they do about how to wire up circuits to get a lamp to light or a buzzer to buzz.

They are also likely to recognize that while a lot of scientific information is relatively certain there is a limit to that certainty, and there are only a limited number of types of question that can be answered within science.

Appreciating the cultural significance of science

Appreciating the cultural significance of scientific knowledge requires some historical perspective, or at least a willingness to recognize that scientific ideas taken for granted today have not always been so. Most people are familiar today with the phrase 'spaceship earth', i.e. an earth as just one member of a universe, not something distinct from the 'heavens'. The earth is accepted as a place where you have only the resources which happen to be on your spaceship. Newton, in recognizing that the behaviour of the apple was governed by the same forces as the behaviour of the moon, contributed significantly to our acceptance of the earth as part of the universe, not separate from the heavens.

The recycling of matter, from water in the atmosphere to water in our bodies, from the carbon in our tissues to the carbon dioxide in the air, from the nitrogen in Aristotle's muscles to the nitrogen in broad beans today, owes much to the work of many chemists down the ages. We are becoming increasingly familiar with living with this idea of recycling, such that the cherished belief of the uniqueness of the individual is understood today partly in terms of the transmission of a unique pattern of information in the genes, not as the uniqueness of the particular material in our construction.

The ability in the twentieth century both to understand and to intervene in the many processes which occur on 'spaceship earth' has raised ethical issues of a dimension which was not faced before: when to give medical treatment and when not; who should control the supply of spare parts for surgery; who should decide about fertility treatment; who should decide when and where cars may be driven? . . .

Thinking about where and how science is learnt

Learning about science therefore is learning about what the natural world is like, what it does and what can be done to it. Learning about science involves learning how it can be explained and coming to grips with some of the 'imagined entities' (current, genes, electrons). It involves appreciating the way in which evidence is collected, locating this knowledge within everyday events, recognizing that science provides tentative answers to only a limited range of all the questions that people might ask, and being aware that scientific knowledge and understanding are inextricably linked to every other aspect of our culture.

Turning from what is learnt in science, to how and where it is learnt, is important. Formal education in schools and colleges will play a part but so will a range of informal learning outside these institutions. The six years in primary school (the focus of the case studies in Part 2) must be seen within a wider and longer continuum of learning.

Informal learning

Much informal learning of science develops from just being in a society where scientific knowledge exists, where technical equipment and processes are available. Considerable knowledge is built up outside formal education: through hobbies, through medical encounters, through reading instructions on technical goods; by knowing that certain things are possible (travelling round the earth in a satellite, using mobile phones to all corners of the earth, knowing that hips can be replaced, having water and electricity automatically in homes); by watching television programmes; by reading books and magazines; by interacting with the material world through construction activities; from science fiction . . .

By the time that children come to school they already have five years of experience of finding out about the material and natural world; they have encountered a lot of technical gadgets, watched television, looked in books, asked questions and had a range of responses, and come up with their own conjectures about some phenomena. This informal learning will continue while they are at school and interact with the science they learn there.

Formal education: learning in school

Formal education provides rather different contexts. The obvious one is that activities are planned with the intention that learning should be the outcome (learning may be the incidental outcome of a trip to a museum with the family, but general motivation and enjoyment may be the primary objectives). Time and physical resources for learning science are allocated in schools; teachers expect to play a significant part in the learning process by their interactions with the learners.

It is difficult to give a general picture of what the provision for science would be like in any school, especially at primary level, despite the common framework of the National Curriculum. This is partly because of the autonomy of schools and of individual teachers to interpret the National Curriculum in their own ways. It is also because schools and teachers have their own personal histories; some schools have had science as an intrinsic part of the curriculum for over 50 years, others have only reluctantly and slowly incorporated it since 1989 with the implementation of the National Curriculum. Similarly some individual teachers had incorporated the study of the natural world as part of their teaching, since they started teaching; others are reluctantly coming to terms with the requirements of a National Curriculum which has made science a 'core subject', hence compulsory.

The National Curriculum in science at primary level contains some of the ten elements of 'knowing some science'. Children are expected to learn about plants and animals as living things which have the same life processes – growing, reproducing, feeding, moving, respiring, etc.; about living organisms as parts of communities within a particular environment and the interactions of the different organisms within the environment; about the properties, behaviour and structure of matter; about physical phenomena such as electrical circuits, sources of energy, forces, sound and light; the place of the earth in the universe. The National Curriculum gives an indication of the facts to be known, the explanations to be understood and the concepts to be learnt (DFE 1995).

Children are expected to learn how to undertake explorations and investigations and how to interpret data, from the actual experience of undertaking experiments and investigations and interpreting the data. Schools, by and large, have the necessary resources and materials for children to engage in such practical activities. These resources tend to be 'low tech' and apart from a few items, are different in character from the equipment typically found in the laboratories in secondary schools. Secondary sources such as books, videos, TV are important for science, supplementing the first-hand experience gained through practical work.

Something of the spirit of 'science in everyday life', 'appreciating the nature of science' and 'appreciating the cultural significance of science' is contained in the National Curriculum, even at primary level. It is hoped that the involvement in finding out about the natural world, through talk, listening, reading and experimenting will allow these understandings to develop.

The National Curriculum stresses the importance of children learning the vocabulary associated with science and the means of representing and displaying data and information, using diagrams, graphs, tables and charts in order to communicate their ideas. What gets almost no mention is the importance of learners making their ideas and constructing their own meanings through the use of language and pictures.

The case studies in Part 2 give an indication of what might be found in practice within formal education and hence provide examples of the way in which the National Curriculum can be interpreted in the classroom. They provide glimpses of what learning in science can be like in the formal context of primary schools and how that learning contributes to the picture of children 'knowing some science'.

Curricula, textbooks and case studies are not the only sources of relevant information about teaching and learning science. Research in science education, much of which has been directed to primary science in the last 30 or 40 years, can also prove useful. In order to tap this research resource I have drawn on published reports from relatively large projects, namely: the Children's Learning in Science project, CLIS (Leeds University) and related studies; the Science Process and Concept Exploration project, SPACE (King's College, London and Liverpool University); Science Teacher Action Research project, STAR (Liverpool University); the Assessment of Performance Unit, APU (national); Procedural and Conceptual Knowledge in Science, PACKS (York and Durham Universities).

Research into young children learning science

Rather than treat each of the ten facets of 'knowing science' separately I have grouped them into three main clusters: the first is
concerned with knowing and understanding facts, explanations
and concepts, and asking questions; the second with understanding experiments, interpreting data and developing technical know-
how; the third with science and everyday life, the nature of science
and the cultural significance of science. To date, research has only
addressed the first two clusters to any significant extent.

Research into knowing about the natural and made world; understanding explanations; developing scientific concepts; and asking questions

Much of the research in this area has focused on how children
'picture' the natural and material world. How do they imagine
light? What do they imagine that it does and where it is? How
do they explain phenomena like how they hear the sound of a
drum, the growth of a plant from a seed, the drying of a towel,
the positions of organs inside the body...

Research on *Children's Learning in Science* began in the late 1960s,
and flourished in the 1970s and early 1980s. CLIS was the acronym for the project at Leeds, but there has been work in this field
worldwide. It has provided a wealth of information about what
children say about a wide range of natural phenomena, what they
expect to happen, how they explain natural events, and their interpretation of what people say or write about science. The research
began in the area of physics with secondary school students, but
has spread to other areas of science and to the primary phase
(Driver *et al.* 1985, 1994).

Extracts from a chapter by Gerald Nussbaum (1985) in a book
named *Children's Ideas in Science* (Driver *et al.* 1985) will illustrate
the field. He writes about teaching 8 and 9-year-olds about the
earth in space. He starts by indicating the nature of the journey
that children have to make from the *perceived* world in which
they live (with a flat surface, with 'up' directly above their heads,
'down' directly below their feet, and the sky some considerable
distance above them) to the *conceived* world where the land on
which they stand is really the surface of a sphere, where 'down'
means towards the centre of this sphere and where 'up' is along

a line going from the centre, outwards along a radius and sky is all around them.

Amongst the tools for diagnosing where children are on this journey, Nussbaum asked them to draw pictures of, or talk about, the 'round earth'. He found that responses included reference to curved roads, round mountains, a round island with sea all round it, and a round earth in the sky with the observer standing on a flat earth. He also set them problems where they had to draw what will happen to a ball dropped at different places on the earth's surface. Many responded by drawing the ball going down the paper, not going towards the centre of the earth. Where correct responses were given, he probed understanding further (see Figure 2.1), to reveal that the egocentric view of the world often still persisted.

Nussbaum identified steps in a progression from the egocentric (the perceived world) to geocentric view of the world (the conceived world), but he made no claim that everyone will follow that route, nor how long it will take to make the journey. He does claim that a teacher can make a difference in whether the journey is embarked on and whether some of the more challenging parts are tackled.

What also emerges from this whole area of research is that the ideas are not confined to children. Ideas found in children can be similar to those found in adults, including people who have considerable formal science education such as science graduates.

A few more examples from other topics will illustrate the point. Studies of children's responses to whether a cow, whale, spider, worm or person is an animal or not, revealed that it is not until the age of 17 years that nearly all children are prepared to recognize that it is reasonable to classify a person as an animal (Osborne and Freyberg 1985). This is not surprising because there are frequently notices up which say 'No animals allowed in here', where people are not excluded.

Questions about where water goes to when puddles disappear, or blackboards dry, reveal that the idea that water, once it has evaporated, is somehow still around although invisible, is not easily accepted. Questions about light reveal that many people believe it travels further at night than during the day. This again is not unreasonable because we might see a light such as a firework from a distance of several hundred metres at night but not during the day (Osborne and Freyberg 1985: 10).

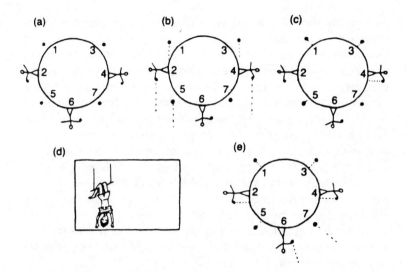

Figure 2.1 A problem situation presented in 'two steps' to detect 'hidden' egocentric views

The child is shown (a) and asked to draw, for positions 1–5 only, lines representing how rocks would fall. Two common alternative responses are given in (b) and (c). If the answer was as in (c) then (d) is shown and the child is asked why the boy's shirt comes to the boy's face. (d) affects some of the children who first responded correctly (c) and they see persons 6 and 7 as standing upside down. Hence they later predict falls to be shown as in (e).

(From Nussbaum 1985: 176)

In the literature, there are a range of views as to the significance of these findings. I would list three:

- science is not a simple extrapolation of the observed world; it is often far from common sense;
- there is a lot to be taught and learnt about a simple statement such as 'the earth is round';
- it is important for teachers to listen to children (or any learner), (and this often means deliberately constructing opportunities for them to elaborate their ideas) so that teachers can appreciate what understanding is already there.

The first point may help to explain why there is still a significant number of primary teachers finding difficulty with the science component of the curriculum. The OFSTED (1995) report on science in the National Curriculum states: 'Some teachers' understanding of particular areas of science, especially the physical sciences, is not sufficiently well developed and this gives rise to unevenness in standards, particularly in Year 5 and Year 6' (pp. 5–6). I often wonder if the difficulty lies more in not understanding the *nature* of the knowledge than in the knowledge itself. Perhaps the relative certainty of scientific knowledge, coupled with what at times has almost become the dogma of 'learning from first-hand experience', has slid over into an unconscious belief that science is obvious and obviously learnt unaided from first-hand experience.

The second point, that there is a lot to teach about the earth being round may seem trivial, but a response to having to teach areas which are unfamiliar is to rush through telling the children a lot of facts without allowing them to 'play' with these facts mentally and see the consequences of the new ideas. Much of the creativity I have talked about in the case studies relates to interesting events and activities that have allowed children to see the 'not so obvious' in the apparently obvious.

I will illustrate the third point about listening and responding appropriately with a conversation I had with a group of infants who were studying the solar system. While they were looking at a photograph of the earth taken from a satellite, I asked them what the picture was. The four all replied that it was the earth and they knew the photograph had been taken from a spaceship. So I asked what the blue was, which was a question that might not have occurred to me had I not read Nussbaum's work. A girl replied that it was the sea, to which, after a short pause, a little boy added 'No, it cannot be the sea because it is up in space.' This was incidentally a boy who could tell me about the names of the planets and quite a lot of factual information about them, but he had not made the connection between the earth he stood on and the earth he saw in a book.

Another relatively large project in primary science, one whose acronym is SPACE, has provided more information about teaching and learning science. The SPACE project (*Science Processes and Concept Exploration*) drew on techniques from CLIS and from APU to research the development of scientific concepts in children for different topics, but it also tried to find out what sort of intervention strategies helped to develop ideas. The team essentially used a pre-test/post-test model of research, testing the children before and after the intervention to see the extent to which ideas had changed. Their 'tests' involved interviews with a selected sample of the classes, but also analysis of products such as children's writing and drawings. They are referred to in the reports as 'elicitation strategies' rather than 'tests'.

An important component of this research was that children were initially given first-hand experience of a practical nature before they were asked what ideas they had. These project reports give details of these exploratory activities which are, in practice, a valuable resource for science teaching. They represent almost a 'play' phase in the learning; the elicitation questions took place in the context of these exploratory activities. For example, the exploratory activities on light are titled:

- Investigating where light comes from.
- How do bicycle reflectors work?
- Investigations with a torch and a mirror.
- Investigations with a torch and paper.
- Looking at candles.
- How do we see?

Details of the torch and mirror activity are given in Figure 2.2. It starts with instructions for the activity, which is in fact a problem, followed by a request for a drawing to show how the problem was solved. Next comes a request for a drawing to explain how the light travels (note that 'travelling' is not something which can be observed but something which has to be imagined). Question 4 asks specifically about the direction of travel and question 5 is pressing for a further explanation of the whole process (i.e. how

Equipment	Torch for each pair of children mirror drawing paper and pencils
Activity	
1	One child holds the torch which is switched on behind the second child's head. The second child is seated and given a plane mirror. He/she is asked to use the mirror to see the light from the torch.
2	Do a drawing to show how you used the mirror to see the light from the torch behind you.
3	Show on the drawing how you think the light travels.
4	Is any light coming towards you?
5	How would you explain what is happening?

Figure 2.2 Torch and mirror activity and the related elicitation questions (Osborne *et al.* 1990, Appendices)

much of the story that the light is leaving the torch, travelling from the torch to the mirror, bouncing off the mirror and travelling into the child's eye, thus enabling him/her to see the torch, can the child give?).

The progression which is evident in this series of instructions and questions is typical of many SPACE interviews. They target specifically scientific ideas (in this case, light as an entity separate from the source; light travels from source outwards; light bounces off a mirror; seeing is associated with light entering the eye), but they also provide the children with activities at the start with which they can easily engage. The findings from the pre-test were then reviewed in order to try to devise 'intervention strategies', i.e. what and how to teach next, in order to develop the children's thinking further. In many cases the intervention strategy was an investigation based on questions children raised in the exploratory phase.

In this topic they explored children's understanding of sources of light and particularly whether they could explain secondary sources; they studied the way children represented light and also their explanations of vision. Only a minority could give a scientific explanation of secondary sources, although there was an improvement towards Year 6. Most children represented light by short rays only, and even after the teaching did not extend the rays any distance from the source. In the matter of vision it was rare for children to indicate the light coming from the source to the object being looked at and then being reflected into the eye. Teaching did make some difference as to whether children indicated links of some sort between the eye and the object and the light source and the object.

Topics in the SPACE project now cover light, earth in space, earth, soils and rocks, electricity, growth, materials, sound, processes of life, genetics and evolution, evaporation and condensation. These have provided a picture of the sort of understandings achieved. I have included examples of findings from two of the other topics, growth and evaporation and condensation.

In the research on growth, the project found that very young children could name sun, water and soil as necessary for growth but rarely named all three and viewed the soil as having a support function only. When a seed grew into a plant, they saw the plant unfolding from the seed, not of it building itself up from material it had taken in. Water was associated with growth and many, even in the junior levels, thought that growth occurred at night. As children got older they did become aware of the span and limit to growth.

In thinking about the growth of a chicken inside an egg the researchers found essentially four different interpretations: one where children thought the body parts were separate and came together just before hatching (this was found only rarely); a second was the idea of the complete animal waiting to be hatched; the third, and commonest, was of a miniature animal structurally complete and feeding to make itself big enough to hatch; the fourth, the transformation of the content of the egg into a structurally refined animal was much rarer. Many children, not surprisingly, thought intuitively that the egg would get heavier as the chicken developed inside the shell.

In the topic on evaporation and condensation, several different contexts were discussed with the children: the reduction of water in a fish tank; clothes drying and a wet handprint on a paper towel disappearing; and evaporation from solutions. In listening to the children's explanations they found that the children used a range of ideas concerning the conservation or non-conservation of water; the change in location of the water; conditions or agents governing change of location; and the nature of the transformation of water (Russell and Watt 1990a: 90). Often the younger children saw no need to explain the disappearance of water, especially in the case of clothes drying, or they explained it in terms of the water falling to the ground. Older children were more inclined to use a 'soaking in' explanation. The loss of water from the tank was often interpeted by the youngest children as the water having leaked away or someone having taken it.

Overall the project provides information for many of the topics in the primary science curriculum, about possible explanations teachers will meet and the likelihood of their being developed into a more scientific set of ideas.

Moving from children's understanding to their ability at 'asking scientific questions' we find there has been relatively little systematic research on the scale of these other projects. There has however been considerable thoughtful commentary on the sort of questions that are needed for science (How many? How often? How long? Which is the better/faster/strongest . . . ? What will happen if . . . ? How do you make something do something? How does that happen? Why does that happen?) and also on ways of generating them in the classroom. In her account 'Helping children raise questions – and answering them', Sheila Jelly wrote from her experience of many different classrooms, about the sorts of questions children ask, and the difficulty of using these productively (Jelly 1985: 47–55). Often the very focused questions needed for science are not asked spontaneously. She discusses how teachers can work from children's spontaneous questions to what she calls 'productive' questions:

> a child's curiosity often does not show itself as spontaneous questioning, but rather as a statement of interests. 'Look it (snail) has little eyes on stalks.' In situations like this, teachers have to intervene in order to frame problems that children can investigate in a scientific way: 'Are they really eyes?' 'Can snails see?' 'How might we find out?' So in practice it is very often a teacher's questioning, not a child's that initiates scientific activity. For this reason any consideration of handling children's questions in science must be closely related to the way in which a teacher handles her own questioning.
>
> (Jelly 1985: 47)

Jos Elstgeest has written extensively on the importance of 'encounters' between children and phenomena (Elstgeest 1985a, 1992, Elstgeest and Harlen 1990) in enhancing their ability to ask questions, and much of his writing is about the sort of encounters that intrigue and puzzle and hence encourage the asking of questions. Elstgeest also gives an important reminder that questions may not come in the verbalized form recognized by adults as questions; someone picking up an object and looking at it in an interested way is a form of question; someone pausing and frowning may indicate that some sort of puzzle has occurred to them; a statement said in a tentative voice may be a question.

Other writers who have focused quite extensively on the problem of helping children to ask and answer questions, bringing together many of the strategies that teachers have found productive are Elstgeest 1985b, Feasey and Thomas 1993, Ollerenshaw and Ritchie 1994, Harlen 1995.

Understanding experiments; interpreting data

In addition to the research into children's ideas, and the commentary on their asking questions, there has been considerable work done in the field of children undertaking investigations. How do they respond to evidence, especially that which is generated in investigations in school? What do they notice? What do they see as significant?

The *Assessment of Performance Unit* was established in the late 1970s as a national body to survey learning in several subjects, including science, of 11, 13 and 15-year-olds. It produced imaginative exercises to find out about students' knowledge and understanding in science, their ability to make measurements, to process scientific data and to plan and undertake investigations. These exercises were used with several thousands of students. This work laid the foundation of much of the early work on the National Curriculum in science (DES 1989), as well as providing tools for the assessment of science and, in the primary field, information about what children could do and understand in science at the age of 11 years (Harlen 1983). Analytical work on the stages of investigations showed how performance in 'planning and doing' was much higher than in 'interpreting data and evaluating'. It also showed the importance of context on the way investigations were undertaken (a problem about the rate of dissolving of a sweet was tackled differently from the same problem set as the rate of dissolving of sugar). The researchers also found that conceptual understanding affected design of investigations (Black 1990: 21) (children who believed that cloth keeps something warm by generating heat, tested materials for the best cloth for wintry conditions by wrapping the cloth round a thermometer). A review of the APU findings most appropriate for primary schools (age 11) is given in Russell *et al.* (1988).

In the late 1980s STAR (*Science Teacher Action Research*) studied children in classrooms, using an observation schedule which focused on the 'process skills' of science. In particular it tried to pick up the effect of teacher intervention as well as build up a picture of the processes in which children were engaged. At the end of the first year the analyses of the results were shared with the teachers, who subsequently focused their teaching to enhance processes not being developed and who became involved in the classroom observation themselves (teachers were paired for this).

The focus of much of the research was on how to assess children while they are working, a task which many teachers find difficult. The identification of the 'clusters' of processes which occur at different stages of investigations is useful in this context (Russell and

Harlen 1990: 84, 85), because the clusters show that there is no need to be observing all the processes at the same time. ('Start up cluster' comprises observing, hypothesizing, planning, raising questions, measuring; the 'planning and doing cluster' involves planning, doing, critical reflection, measuring, manipulating variables, observing and recording; the 'interpreting cluster' involves recording, interpreting, communicating – critical reflection, hypothesizing can lead to new investigations. See Figure 2.3). In addition one of the spin-offs of the research for other teachers is the collection of examples of what a hypothesis, prediction, etc. looks like from a 9-year-old's point of view or, indeed, from any

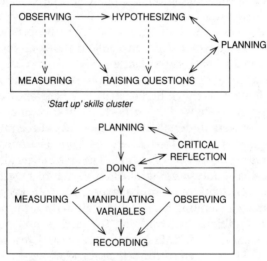

'Start up' skills cluster

'Planning and doing' skills cluster

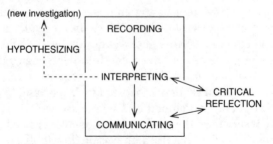

The 'interpreting' cluster of process skills

Figure 2.3 Clusters of skills in investigations (Russell and Harlen 1990: 82–4)

age-group standpoint that is recorded in the books (Russell and Harlen 1990).

One of the findings of this and other research (subsequent work at Durham (Foulds *et al.* 1992), and antecedents in the APU work), is that while children undertake investigations, they do not, as a rule, record data, measure carefully, consider their evidence, try to use their evidence to answer the question, nor evaluate their methods, without intervention from the teacher. A book that gives ideas of how to help children develop these skills is Rosemary Feasey's and Anne Goldsworthy's book on investigations (Goldsworthy and Feasey 1994). It has a range of exercises closely related to investigations, which a teacher can use to help children think about aspects of an investigation without the teacher having to generate the information themselves.

A further more recent project, PACKS (*Procedural and Conceptual Knowledge in Science*), investigated the approaches children take to investigations, as well as the development and evolution of these approaches over the age range 8–13 years. The phrase 'procedural knowledge' acknowledges that the notion of evidence, the notion of a fair test, should be treated as knowledge that has to be understood. It explored how the way in which children tackle investigations (i.e. proceed) is linked to their understanding of the procedures and to their conceptual understanding of the topic in hand (Millar *et al.* 1994). PACKS devised 'concept and data probes' related to each investigation. The concept probes find out about children's concepts related to the subject and have similarities with material used to elicit pupils' ideas such as in the CLIS and SPACE project. The data probes judge pupils' ability to interpret data, to decide whether differences between measurements are significant or not, and in what circumstances repeated measurements should be made.

One important element of the PACKS research was the categorization of investigation modes that children adopt, which were described respectively as:

- the engagement frame
- the modelling frame
- the engineering frame
- the scientific frame.

These can be illustrated by reference to one of the problems, 'Cool bag', in which children had to investigate how the thickness of padding affects how well a cool bag works. In the engagement frame children do something with the equipment that is provided but what they do bears little relationship to the question. In the modelling frame children make something which visually resembles features of a problem rather than relating to significant variables; in this case they selected equipment and materials that were as near as possible to the shape of the cool bag in the picture. In the engineering frame they used the material to make the best cool bag they could. In the scientific frame they took measurements for different numbers of layers of cloth and made decisions about how the thickness affected the inside temperature.

As so often happens, analysis like this raises awareness of events seen but not registered. 'That's fascinating,' said a teacher who had read the PACKS report, 'only yesterday I saw an example of the modelling frame where a child made a horseshoe magnet out of Plasticine and couldn't understand why it wouldn't work.' And other teachers have said, 'Yes, that's right, people get on with an investigation – especially if the equipment is there – but often tackle it differently from the way you expect or answer a totally different question.'

Research and teaching

The link between research and teaching is elusive and yet all the teachers involved in these and other research projects found that their practice in the classroom was significantly altered as a result. Below is an extract from the SPACE project:

> Teachers had commented in an earlier meeting that the role expected of them was one that they were not used to. The work required that teachers should be less judgmental than normal and gave children an opportunity to discuss and express their ideas without criticism from the teacher. In addition, the emphasis placed by the project on conceptual development was one that was unfamiliar to the teachers.
>
> Osborne *et al.* 1990: 31

The involvement in research of the STAR project was reported by all the teachers to be of value in understanding what they were aiming for in their classes and being able to identify significant events and products. The detailed analysis of the process skills, with an indication of ways of judging progression in them were much valued.

Many of the teachers used as 'testers' for the APU practical tasks similarly reported the way in which the involvement and training as researchers had increased their ability to notice events which were important indicators of the children's learning, which they would previously have missed.

I think that it is no coincidence that several (but not all) of the teachers whose case studies appear had read reports of research of this kind. The reading helped alert them to the significance of what children were saying and to techniques which they could use to elicit and extend understanding.

Summary

The research in science education provides insights into the constraints and possibilities in learning science in primary schools which we can use to view the case studies. What happened in the classrooms may replicate the findings of the research; they may conflict with the findings. Where research shows certain areas of learning as difficult, then it is important to see how teachers have managed to support children in that learning and the extent to which they have had success.

The goals of science education also provide a framework through which to view the learning; does the science taught in these schools relate to this wider interpretation of science education or has primary science some other agenda?

Part 2

CASE STUDIES

Part 2

CASE STUDIES

3

Parks, woods and wastelands

YEARS 3 AND 4 (7 TO 9-YEAR-OLDS)

The jigsaw of teaching

Writing about classroom practice proved more challenging than I had anticipated when I embarked on this book. A first attempt at this chapter produced a chronological account, with commentary and rationale, which was accurate and informative, but dull. Eventually I came to use the metaphor of a jigsaw puzzle to guide the writing, because it seemed to me that I often learnt about other people's teaching rather like someone finding the picture in their puzzle: piece by piece, building up a section here, one there and then finding pieces that linked one section with another, until finally almost all the puzzle is complete save for a few pieces which lie unnoticed on the table. At the end these last stray pieces fit effortlessly into empty spaces and take on new meaning.

The pieces for the jigsaw of this chapter were collected in several ways. First, the teacher, Anne Robertson, had presented many of them in her written account and analysis of her teaching. All otherwise unattributed quotations are from this source. Second, a conversation with her two years later when I started writing this chapter provided further pieces. Third, I learnt at that time that her current Years 3 and 4 class were studying the same topic and that she was using many of the ideas she had developed previously. I therefore visited her class and stayed for over an hour photographing events, displays and the wildlife area in the grounds. Fourth, having omitted to photograph 'Professor Sense', a key player in the drama, I returned to record him and inevitably to find more pieces. Fifth, the first draft of the chapter was given to the teacher who corrected it and added more linking pieces.

Metaphors have their limits. It is impossible to collect, let alone present in the space of a small book, all the linking pieces in the jigsaw of teaching. In this class were 28 children aged 8 or 9 years old, each with their own histories and personalities. Conversations and relationships between them, and between them and their teacher, are part of the jigsaw which, save for a few instances, have not been and cannot be captured. There is the personal professional history of this particular teacher, the ethos and the history of the school, the families from which the children come; all are pieces which are relevant but in the main unreported. The reader must imagine or at least surmise about them.

An overview of the topic

I have provided a chronological outline of the whole of the topic at the end of the chapter in Figure 3.7. The reader, like the person who chooses to turn the lid of the jigsaw for guidance, may find it helpful to turn to these pages occasionally and fit the episodes into the whole picture. The organization of the outline into five stages, each subdivided into 'planning' and 'assessment', is the teacher's and not mine; she was interested at the time to research and reflect upon the interaction between planning and formative assessment in her teaching.

There are references in the text to groups A, B and C. Group A contained children who were still having difficulties in reading and writing and on the whole were slow in learning. Group B had reasonably developed reading and writing skills, but were less articulate than C. This latter group were confident and fluent writers and readers and could put ideas into spoken words with considerable confidence.

A park, a wood and a wasteland were within easy reach of the school. The wasteland available was a piece of derelict land (20 metres by 10 metres) behind the cinema not far from the school. The park was within ten minutes walk, while the woodland, Epping Forest, was five miles away, where a coach trip was necessary.

The teacher's objectives were that children should become more knowledgeable and inquisitive about the local environment, that they should be able to ask and investigate their own questions, and that they should develop their knowledge and understanding both of living things within a range of habitats and of the interrelationships between living things.

She spent five to six hours a week on the topic for half a term, giving about 40 hours of teaching altogether. Much of the development of language, maths and art were merged with the science, so the five to six hours covered more than science. There was no science topic in the second half of the term; the 40 hours was, therefore, the time devoted to science over the whole term.

The pieces I found in the jigsaw were classroom stories, interactive displays, visits to the park, woodland and wasteland, assessment schedules, pro formas for investigations, letters to the council about rubbish on the wasteland, concept maps, a box which the teacher kept knocking on to the floor thus spilling its contents, pictures of two professors, databases on invertebrates, drawings of minibeasts, a heap of questions asked by the children, children's own investigations, a lot of knowledge about living things and their habitats, conversations about the topic rich in language and detail, and the children's growing confidence that their ideas, questions and reflections were a valued part of classroom life.

The teaching can be viewed in five fairly classical stages:

- brainstorming;
- early explorations, with children beginning to generate questions and extend their knowledge;
- further disciplined activities during which a rich variety of questions were generated by the children and answered by book research;
- practical investigations to find answers to five questions from first-hand evidence;
- consolidation of learning by exploring a more complex environment – Epping Forest.

By the end of the third stage (the phase when a lot of questions were generated, see above) the teacher had achieved her objective that the children should be able to generate good questions; there were 29 good focused questions which indicated a considerable breadth and depth of knowledge. This is impressive by any standard. The story now tracks back to the start of the topic to see how she led up to this point.

The start of the topic

During the initial brainstorming the teacher had asked the whole class to talk about what they thought would be in the topic, and which parks, woods and wasteland they had seen or visited and what they had noticed there. Not surprisingly she found that they knew the wasteland to be a place where people dumped rubbish and where children were told not to play. The children often visited the local park to play on the swings and climbing frames, but had noticed little else there. None of the class had visited a wood or a forest and some muddled 'wood' with 'would'.

She asked the class to think of questions they might try and answer when they visited these places. There were not many; some about what sort of rubbish people dumped on the wasteland and a few about the playing equipment such as: 'How high is the climbing frame?' 'How many steps are there on the slide?' Most of the latter led to mathematics investigations rather than science.

A classroom story and a sensory visit

The first 'sensory visit' to the park was planned and imminent, with the requisite number of other adults booked to go with the class. Productive visits, however, need more than administrative organization: they need the children to be mentally prepared for the exploration ahead. This triggered the telling of a story and this is how it went:

Professor Sense
One Monday morning, the headteacher told all the children during assembly that they would be having a special visitor coming to their classroom that day.
    Later that day the door of our classroom opened and there

stood the most unusual man that the children had ever seen. He smiled, walked in, sat down and invited all the children and the teacher to come and sit beside him. At first, the children stared at him. What they noticed most of all were his eyes which were very large and round. They seemed to be moving round and round slowly all the time. It was almost as if they were on stalks. Next, they noticed his ears. They seemed to move towards the slightest sounds around the room. The children felt vibrations which seemed to come from these. As he spoke to the children, his nose twitched like a rabbit's. Sometimes he crumpled it up as if he didn't like what he could smell. Every now and then, his tongue appeared from between his lips and he seemed to be tasting the very air that they were all breathing. The children noticed that his hands were big and firm but they looked very gentle.

The children were fascinated by this unusual person. As they listened and watched they felt their eyes tingling, their ears vibrating, their noses twitching and their tongues beginning to water. They looked at their hands to see if anything was happening to those and they noticed the lines that they had never seen before.

'Who are you?' asked one little boy. 'I am Professor Sense,' said the unusual visitor, 'would you like to learn with me?'

The story, like many classroom stories which teachers use for explanation, would not have been written down if it were not for the fact that she was researching her own teaching at the time. It was a story which fascinated and intrigued; the children responded enthusiastically to the request that they should draw Professor Sense (Figure 3.1).

Sitting on the grass in the park the teacher reminded the children of Professor Sense and asked them to use all their senses while they were touching the grass. They sustained this in almost complete silence with little difficulty for ten minutes; the tape recorder was then turned on and each child invited to share something sensed. The things that the children described were mostly about the grass – the scratchiness on the back of their legs, that there were several little bits joined together at the bottom of the blades of grass, descriptions of 'waving greenness'. Then the questions began to emerge:

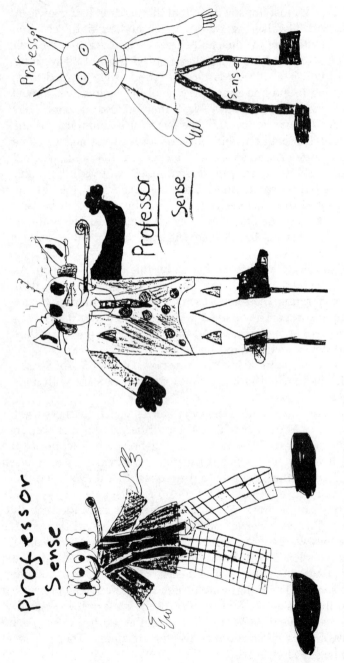

Figure 3.1 Children's drawings of Professor Sense

EA asked 'Is all the grass the same?'
   Some children answered, 'Yes' while others replied, 'No'.
   They then all looked at me. I waited and looked as if I was thinking. Then an idea was expressed.
AG 'We could find out.'
EA 'How?'
SO 'I know, we could all look about and pick one bit then bring it back and put them together and check.'
AG 'Oh yeah, can we try that?'

The teacher has come to recognize that this sort of scenario occurs frequently. It can often lead to group discussion, investigation and research, providing she sticks to her role of:

• waiting for someone else to come up with a response to the first question;
• allowing the children to explore their suggestions at the appropriate level;
• making some response to the discussion in hand, e.g. 'I wonder if there are more types of grass in other places?';
• refraining from extending their knowledge immediately, e.g. by saying that there are innumerable types of grasses that grow in all sorts of different habitats.

She reported:

These, for me, are vital points in the children's development. First, they have the possibility to think and to believe in themselves as having valuable responses. Second, it encourages them to explore ways of finding answers. Third, it allows them to discover the limitations in their investigations, if they are able to, while being respected and not put down. Fourth, it discourages an attitude of believing that the teacher or another adult has all the answers.

During the subsequent search for different grasses, more specific questions were framed and more detailed observations made: 'Are they all grass?' 'Why has this got like little flowers?' 'This one is browny and all those are green' 'These ones are all long', etc. The discussion finished with one child saying: 'Well, there must be different sorts so there's not just grass all the same. Does grass get into books, Miss?' The teacher confirmed that she thought they had books with grasses in, at which one child, a non-reader, asked if they could take grasses back 'to see if our grass is in a book'. (A small selection of grasses were taken back with the appropriate explanation as to why this was permissible when plants should not normally be picked.) This child subsequently spent a long time on several occasions pouring over a book matching up the grasses and wanting to read the relevant information, asking other children to read certain paragraphs for her.

Sorting grasses into various groups, discussing the different characteristics which distinguished one from another, was one task undertaken back at school. This requires attention to small detail as differences between one grass and another are not easy to spot, even though the flower heads on the grasses at that time of the year would have helped.

I pause in the narrative about the teaching to focus on the classroom. Primary classrooms generally look attractive with children's work on the wall, but displays can contribute more to learning by being interactive. My recent visit to the classroom revealed several interactive displays intrinsic to the teaching. By then another Professor Sense had been introduced and was one of six interactive displays.

Interactive displays and another classroom story

The teacher was keen that all displays were ones which require some interaction from the children. There were six of this type in her classroom:

- woodlands
- Professor Question
- folders for categories of questions
- research questions, next to the books
- park designs
- Professor Sense.

The woodland display comprised a large board on which the children stuck their drawings so that a collage of the many living things in a woodland was slowly built up during the topic. An early task was for each child to cut out a tree shape, paint one side as a tree, but write on the other side their ideas about woods and woodlands. These were pinned by one corner only so that the children could turn them over periodically and see for themselves how much they had progressed by reviewing how much more they now knew.

Professor Question was a small box pinned to the wall by the computer, where every now and again a child went and wrote a question, printed it out and 'fed' it to the professor. The display included the words 'How? What? When? Why? Who?' as prompts for starting questions. Only three weeks into the topic I found, in the class I visited, that Professor Question had already been 'fed' those listed below:

How does a snail make its shell?
Is a ladybird a bird?
How many legs has an insect?
What is a caterpillar?
Do earthworms feel dry or wet?
What does an earthworm eat?
What do ladybirds eat?
When do ladybirds get their spots?
What are aphids?
Is a spider an insect?
How many sorts of butterfly can you get?
How many legs has a spider?
Is an ant an insect?
Can a fox eat a bird?
Does an ant lay eggs?

and by the end of the topic she had been fed far more.

Who was Professor Question? She, like Professor Sense, was the figment of the imagination of the teacher, who created her after the success of the story of Professor Sense. This is her story which depicts both the interaction between observation and questioning and how questioning provokes questioning:

Professor Question
All of a sudden, one day, the classroom door burst open. A very unusual person stood there almost as if on one leg and asked, 'Hello. Have you seen my friend? We seem to have lost each other. Now, where do you think he can be? Can you help? I am lost, you see. Can you tell me which way I should go next?'

One girl nearby said, 'Who are you looking for?' A boy said, 'Where do you want to go to?' The teacher moved across the classroom and asked, 'May I help you? Have you been to the office?'

'You may help me if you can, but can you?' replied the unusual person.

'I don't know. Who are you looking for? What do you want?' asked the teacher.

The visitor looked very confused.

The teacher tried again, 'Have you been to the office?'

'Where's the office? Who will I find there? How do I get there?' replied the visitor.

By this time, the teacher looked confused too and the children thought it was a huge joke. The teacher put on a disapproving look. One child, trying to be helpful, asked 'Who are you? Maybe, if we know that we can help you. Who are you?'

At this point, the visitor's face lit up with excitement. 'I can answer that one,' the visitor exclaimed, 'I am Professor Question. Do you know me? Does that help you to help me?'

Another child called out, 'Professor Question! That's unusual. Is that why you keep on asking questions? Who is your friend?'

'Oh dear! You're all catching it, aren't you?'

'Catching what? Is it like measles?' asked another child.

Just at that moment, the classroom door opened again and in walked the children's old friend, Professor Sense. 'Oh, here you are, Question. I wondered where you'd got to. Getting on OK? Pleased you've met my friends. Are they looking after you all right?'

'Please, can someone tell me what is going on?' asked the anxious teacher.

'This is my friend, Professor Question. Usually, we go about together most of the time, you know. I tell her things. She asks questions, don't you dear?'

'Yes, I certainly ask questions. But I don't know about you telling me things. You notice things most of the time, don't you?'

'Yes, that's right. I notice them and I tell you about them and you start asking questions about them and then I have to notice more and tell you and then you ask . . .'

'Yes, yes,' interrupted the teacher, 'I think we've got all that now. Now, where can we go from here?'

At that point the children burst out laughing.

The story helped to reinforce what was meant by a question; the classroom display with its signs saying 'How? When? Where? . . .' was a reminder of words which often signal the start of a question.

The teacher's provision of folders for different types of questions, labelled respectively *'To find out* we can *watch'*, *'To find out* we can *read'*, *'To find out* we can *investigate'*, are an undisguised adoption of ideas that classifying questions should follow collecting questions from Feasey and Thomas (1993). The decision about which categories to use was made as part of a class discussion on ways of finding out answers to the questions, and is another example of an event devised to enable the children to play a significant role in decisions.

The children were in mixed-ability groups for the classification exercise, in order to give 'groups A and B the opportunity of contributing their ideas while benefiting from the reading, writing and investigative skills of group C, and to encourage group C to receive ideas and suggestions from the others and to help them clarify their thinking and planning as they explained it carefully'.

This classification exercise revealed that questions could often go into more than one category – eventually groups had to decide in which category the questions should go. The questions themselves generated a lot of discussion and helped the children clarify their understanding and knowledge of both the content of the questions and of the processes of finding out. The teacher reported that what was becoming evident by this stage was a growing acceptance by the children of there being more than one way of doing things, of the possibility of more than one right answer, and a recognition that some questions may not be able to be answered by the class with the time and resources that they had available. Discussions in the classification exercise generated further questions, such that the collection and classification of questions became concurrent rather than sequential activities. The folders were fed by questions on a regular basis over a week; questions were also removed as children found answers to them from their reading.

By the side of the reference book collection were three lists of questions devised by the teacher. These were, on the whole, either more difficult than some of the ones the children were asking, or they extended the areas studied. They were primarily for the older children (this class had two year groups in it, Years 3 and 4), or for those who were working faster than the others.

One wall contained a large display of park designs for different groups of people (girl of 5, 8-year-old boy, woman of 38, older person). There was an invitation to the children to select the most appropriate design in each category and to sign their names against the ones of their choice. These designs were a development of a map-making exercise which children undertook on their second visit to the park, as a result of which they developed an awareness of the park as a very varied environment, with grass areas, flower beds, bush areas. The play area was only a tiny part of it all.

Professor Sense had been developed further into an interactive box. This box became a repository for 'sense sentences', i.e. any statements which described observations (for example, 'the road is noisy'). The teacher had also told the story to an infant class and made Professor Sense into a 'feely box' for them.

Interactive displays of the sort described here allow children to engage in an activity over time, to view their progress by watching displays grow (question box; question folders), to reflect and make up their minds without being hurried (decisions about the park), and to have something to do if they complete work quickly (questions by the side of the reference books). They also provide the teacher with the opportunity to start an activity in a formal, controlled way with the whole class together, while accommodating subsequently the different learning speeds and strategies of the children in her class.

In the case of the questions, the display matched the way in which questions often arise from other activities, and as it was there waiting to be fed, a child did not have to break off from something else for long to feed in the question. The close observation and building of a database were two of the activities which stimulated the production of questions.

Close observation and building a database

The drawings in Figure 3.2 and the information tables on minibeasts (Figure 3.3) came from two closely related activities. The teacher used work on minibeasts to develop children's observational skills. The study was highly structured in many ways. The children had collected minibeasts from the park and from the school grounds and these were kept in a tank in the classroom. Children selected one and were asked to:

Figure 3.2 Children's drawings of minibeasts

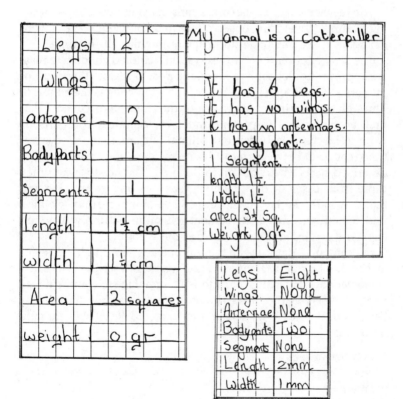

Legs	12
Wings	0
antenne	2
Body Parts	1
Segments	1
length	1½ cm
width	1¼ cm
Area	2 squares
weight	0 gr

My anmal is a caterpiller

It has 6 Legs.
It has NO wings.
It has no antennaes.
1 body part.
1 Segment.
length 1½.
width 1¼.
area 3½ Sq.
Weight 0g'r

Legs	Eight
Wings	None
Antennae	None
Bodyparts	Two
Segments	None
Length	2mm
widti	1mm

Figure 3.3 Data on minibeasts

- draw the minibeast;
- write five facts about it, from observation;
- share observations with others.

Drawing is a form of investigation – it holds the drawer's attention and makes them look and re-look endless numbers of times. Detail of how and where one part is joined to another is noticed, the relative lengths and numbers of parts, the shapes and colours. The children used magnifying glasses to see and understand detail, and observation grids to help them get relative sizes sorted out; they used various media to portray these, e.g. pencil, charcoal, pastels and paint.

It is always impressive how much people learn about something from drawing it, so that writing five facts about the creature afterwards was relatively straightforward.

The teacher's role is also important in asking questions, noticing features, developing observations and knowledge, e.g. 'I wonder what those antennae do? They're moving all the time.'

The activity of sharing the observations required children to master appropriate descriptive language and to realize the value of numerical description (How many legs? How long is the animal?). Through the sharing of observations the children discovered that first, accuracy was important and that second, if comparisons were to be made between one animal and another, or observations checked between two observers, then the characteristics described had to be common to them all. The need for accuracy came from cases of disagreement, such as one group claiming that a woodlouse had eight legs, while another group claimed that it had six. The disagreement led quite naturally to going back and having a detailed look at the woodlice.

Building up a database on the computer, where specific descriptors had to be put in, reinforced the need for describing the same characteristics. Selecting characteristics on which to comment was relatively easy as they were drawn from the various characteristics that different groups had chosen to record. The list eventually used was:

number of legs
wings
antennae
body parts
segments

length
width
area
weight.

While the children were undertaking this observational work, the teacher drew attention to life cycles and asked them to research from books the life cycles of the animals they found. The class also followed the development of a colony of caterpillars that they found in the school grounds.

Classification box – the need for repetition

Figure 3.7 at the end of the chapter shows that classification of animals was introduced during the third stage of the teaching. The box that the teacher kept 'accidentally' knocking on the floor was the 'classification box', containing pictures of animals, which needed resorting as a result of the 'accident' – an interesting way of building in the need for repetition in learning.

What might be taught about classification to children of this age? Probably that it is useful to group animals with sufficiently similar characteristics so that it is possible to know something about the group without knowing about every individual within the group; and that groups can be divided into subgroups. What is also important is that much of the classification which is used for biological material uses types of life cycle as well as structure to separate out different groups. Hence learning about life cycles was necessary for learning about classification.

The teacher introduced the idea of classification from the work on databases, which had enabled the children to spot similarities and differences between animals. What they found particularly difficult was the idea of groups within groups. She devised a series of boxes, Russian doll-style, so that when children were sorting animals into groups, they could first divide them into two big groups (vertebrate and invertebrate) and then into smaller and smaller groups. Inside the vertebrate box, there would be smaller boxes for mammals, fishes, birds, amphibians and reptiles. A picture of a dog would then go into the mammal box, which would be put in the vertebrate box.

Once the set of boxes had been established and a few games

had been played with the whole class, the children benefited immensely from it. It became the source of much discussion, many questions and several games. The speech therapist used it on several occasions in order to encourage children to describe animals using characteristics which enabled another child to work out which animal was being described. The children invented many games themselves. The use of scientific terminology improved; children used words like 'insect', 'arachnid', 'mollusc', 'invertebrate' accurately, without hesitation, and were able to compare groups by their characteristics.

Children talking – cooperation

The teacher in this case study places a high value on children learning to communicate well orally and to cooperate with other people. She builds opportunities for these into as many activities as possible. Her organization is such that she frees herself to be able to talk to and listen to the children.

She monitors progress in talking and reported that children were eager to talk about their pictures of Professor Sense and explain why they had put various features in them:

> Members of group A each spoke several consecutive sentences in an animated way to me about their ideas. They asked to share it with a parent who works with them each day. Later in the week when the speech therapist came for this lesson, they repeated the same request . . . They do not like speaking and have been worried by it in the past.

When three boys presented their drawing of a cross-section of the tube of a trapdoor spider in its hole, she asked them about the shape of the hole. 'What would you use if you wanted to make a model of it?' 'What is that shape called?', . . . etc.

The tape which the children had started on their first sensory walk to the park was often replayed and added to during the topic. It is not easy to do this in a busy classroom where other noises can interfere with the tape. The teacher organized recording by individuals during the 20-minute silent reading period which they had every day after lunch. One child was allowed to go into the teacher's cupboard and record, during this period, without disturbing the class and without extraneous noises being picked up by the microphone.

Investigating their own questions

The teacher had set as an objective that children should investigate questions that they had generated themselves, i.e. ones that
they were likely to understand and to be interested in. The class
selected five investigable questions:

* Where do worms like to live?
* What makes a good home for an ant?
* What lives in a tree?
* What flowers do bees like best?
* What leaves do aphids like to eat most?

and each group chose three to investigate.

The detail from 'Where do worms like to live?' has been used
here to show the sort of investigation that was achieved and also
how the teacher enabled the children to make as many decisions
as possible, themselves. The children decided to select three areas
and find out in which one they could find the most worms. They
chose a soil area; the grass; and in the bushes in front of the school
car park. They had to be taught how to get worms out of the
ground, by pouring on a very mild soap solution, but apart from
that the planning was the children's.

One group at a time went into the school grounds. At the planning stage just as the first group was going out, one child asked,
'When do we have to come back?' As on many other occasions
the teacher handed the responsibility for the decision to the children. 'How long do you think you need?' was the reply, and the
group had no difficulty in setting a sensible time limit. Then finally
before they left she asked for a prediction: 'Have you any idea
where you will find the most worms?' The answer from three
children was 'On the grass', and from the other three 'In the soil'.
They argued that they would not find worms in the bush area by
the car park because of the 'smoke from teachers' cars'.

It was not long before one of the group returned asking for
measuring equipment to ensure the areas used were the same in
the three locations. The need for measuring had become apparent while they were on the job. What was particularly valuable
about this was that children from groups A and B were able to
explain to the next group how to make the measurements.

The actual findings were that the bush area had the most worms, the soil next and the grass least. The teacher prompted a discussion of why that might be and the children willingly offered sensible and plausible explanations. 'Perhaps children in the area affect it. We think that perhaps worms don't like children, but we do not know what they do like. Can we try it in the park on our next visit?'

As already mentioned, the teacher is particularly skilled in having time to talk with children about the work in hand. Very few of her conversations with children are about organization. She therefore plays an essential role of 'lifting thinking' by asking probing questions. She encouraged children to discuss what they were doing and thinking at every stage and asked questions which helped them clarify their ideas. The investigation became a series of events, each one followed by discussion. For the next few weeks a pattern continued of planning, discussing; investigating, discussing; recording and evaluating, discussing.

Because the groups had to undertake three investigations the teacher noticed that during this time:

- children developed a method of writing their plan systematically;
- they grew in independence of thought and action;
- their hypotheses became more detailed and reasoned, e.g. 'I think that ants prefer to live under logs because other animals that eat them can't find them as easily as on a tree';
- they recognized more easily when they were not answering their original questions;
- they became more confident about methods of recording;
- they were more able to evaluate their methods of working.

They seemed to grow to trust that they would not be told off if they said that the work did not go well and became confident to search for reasons and to share these reasons.

Letters to the council

The personal involvement and understanding that was generated in this topic resulted in the writing of letters to the council about the state of the wasteland, which incidentally was later cleared of most of the rubbish.

Consolidation

The visit to Epping Forest was the culmination of the project. The autonomy of the children by this time was such that they decided beforehand for themselves which of their questions they were going to follow up in the woodland and what investigations they were going to do. They prepared the necessary data sheets. It rained that day, but nevertheless the visit went ahead. Data sheets had to be put away on the coach, as a result, and they 'went on an adventure'. They were fascinated by fungi, especially on fallen trees – and asked lots of questions. They enjoyed the atmosphere; they often stood and listened and watched quietly. Many animals – fox, squirrel, innumerable frogs – were seen and they did several investigations but they had to remember data. They acknowledged the inaccuracy of this procedure later in their written accounts.

Several offered explanations for their findings, e.g. 'I think I found more worms because there was good soil for them, plenty of places to hide from their enemies, and not many people walked there so they did not get squashed much.'

Formative assessment

Assessment checklists

To help keep track of the children's development, in both their observation and investigation skills, the teacher devised the checklists shown in Figures 3.4 and 3.5. The observation checklist focuses on the level of detail which is observed, the use of the senses, the skill with a hand lens, the ability to group similar observations in a classification exercise, the ability to describe observations in words and drawings, and the ability to recognize patterns. The scale from 'beginning' to 'competent' is useful because it implies skills and understanding that grow over time.

The investigation checklist requires little comment – it has all the stages of an investigation (see Chapter 2) and allows the teacher to record both oral and written contributions from the children.

Considering questions

Any classroom product (writing, speech, drawings, models, actions) provides useful information if the teacher is able to be analytical.

OBSERVATION CHECKLIST

	Beginning	Developing	Competent
Observes gross features			
Observes detail			
Observes fine detail			
Observes differences			
Observes similarities			
Uses all relevant senses			
Observes sequences of events			
Can use a hand lens			
Can sort and classify as result of observation			
Can describe observations			
Can recognize patterns in observations			

Figure 3.4   Observation checklist

The questions, for instance, that children wrote soon after Professor Question was introduced provided useful insight into their development at that point. Group A could ask questions but not write them down. Their questions tended to be fairly general: 'What animals do you find in the park?' 'What can you see in a forest?' 'Why is there a forest?', which indicated that they needed more experience in simple observations in order to build up a better knowledge of these places. Group B asked similar questions, mostly concerned with the difference between parks, woods and wastelands, but they could write. Group C were already asking questions of a more specific nature about life in the places, several of which had the potential to lead to investigations: 'What do trees do for us?' 'Why do ants like trees?' 'What is soil?'.

Concept maps

The concept maps shown in Figure 3.6 were drawn in July near the end of the topic, and again were a product that gave feedback to

INVESTIGATION CHECKLIST

	Beginning	Developing	Competent
HYPOTHESIZING Mentions 1 relevant feature in explanation			
Mentions > 1 relevant feature			
Gives a logical explanation			
PLANNING Aware of fair test			
Identifies appropriate variable			
Identifies keep same			
Identifies equipment necessary			
MEASURE Makes comparison			
Uses appropriate unit			
Takes adequate measure			
INTERPRETATION Offers related to data			
Checks new data			
Notices pattern in data			
RECORDING Clear, consistent method			
Accurate oral			
Accurate written			
Use of chart/graph			
EVALUATE Can offer improvement			
Notices flaws			

Figure 3.5 Investigation checklist

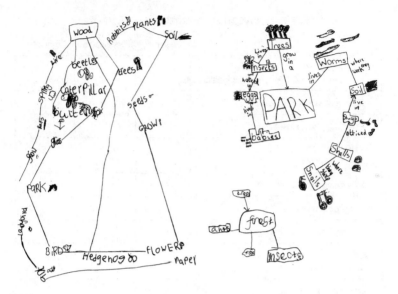

Figure 3.6   Concept maps (draft)

the teacher about what the children understood and what they could put down in writing and drawing that expressed their understanding.

Development of knowledge

I asked the teacher to describe the concepts she had hoped to develop and the sort of understanding she thought the children have of each concept. Below is a summary of her response.

Life cycle: Each group of animals 'wants' to continue, so they have to have babies which will grow up. By the end of the topic children were able to talk about the life cycle of several animals which they found.

The notion of life cycle became extended to plants, with children slowly realizing that many of them had seeds or some other structure which grew into the next plant – trees have come from seeds; bulbs grow into next year's plants.

Classification: To begin with children classified animals according to external features, so that birds and butterflies were put together because they could both fly, worms and slugs were paired together, because of the similar shapes of their bodies. Cats and dogs were put together because they were pets. The more they researched the animals the more they were able to identify other features which were similar. Snails and slugs were seen to be related. Cats and dogs were put into a larger group of mammals as animals that give birth to live young as opposed to laying an egg. They learnt that insects are a large group of animals, all of which have six legs. They also learnt that for invertebrates it was useful to record information about legs, wings, antennae, body parts, segments, size (length, width, area and weight).

Diversity of living things: Grass was obviously the first eye-opener here; there was more than one type of grass, and then when the children looked carefully, a grassy area was made up of many plants other than grass. The diversity of minibeasts found was impressive (several sorts of spiders, caterpillars, ants, woodlice, slugs, snails . . .).

Habitats: Children became aware that different things lived in different places, so that animals living under a log are different from those living in the pond. The problems that they had with the inter-habitat animals which could be found at two places (e.g. a frog) made them realize that habitats were not tightly bounded.

The park was seen at the start as 'a place to play in' but by the end of the topic was seen as a place with many habitats (the grass, the borders, etc.).

They started with the idea that a tree was just a tree – and ended realizing that under the tree, on the tree, up there at the top were different habitats for different creatures.

Needs/characteristics of living things: The fact of animals needing to eat and to breathe and to move to find the things they need was not too difficult. The idea of plants needing food is more difficult. Children of this age can believe that a plant gets much of what it needs from the soil (water in particular) but not that it needs something from the air. They cannot see the air let alone have an idea that it is made up of different components (although the fact that many children have asthma and hayfever makes them aware of things, such as pollen, in the air which might cause their breathing difficulties).

Food chain: This is a difficult idea. They often get so carried away drawing a food chain that imagination takes over from reality. (People eating dogs and dogs eating eagles . . . !) However, once when the class had snails on the ground and there were birds circling overhead, one child said 'I wonder if they are coming for the snails and want to eat them?' – so some notion of food chain related to first-hand evidence was registering.

Decay: The children understood this as a long slow process, recognizing that things changed over time, e.g. horse droppings. They looked at things that people dropped: some decayed, some did not.

Summary – one morning's visit

There are many pieces to this jigsaw. They fit together and represent a highly developed and well thought-out teaching plan. There was, however, something almost unremarkable on entering the classroom. The class were working busily and relatively quietly when I visited. The children had all watched a video tape first thing in the morning about animals in various habitats and about animals building homes at specific times. Several were busy answering questions about the tape from the information books. One group was drawing a trapdoor spider from a book and discussing what the book said about it. Many were on the maths problem associated with leaves, and every now and again a child would go and collect a leaf from the school grounds. Once in a while a child would get up and write a question for Professor Question, print it off and feed it in. Some children completed paintings of trees or leaves and left them to dry. At the end of the morning the children tidied the books away, organized their desks and left for play. Two tearful arguments had also been sorted out. The teacher moved systematically from group to group working alongside the children and moving their thinking forward at every opportunity.

When I returned again two or three weeks later, the parks poster had been replaced by the work on minibeast acrostics and several of the other classroom displays had been changed – showing an ever-changing educational environment for the children in this class.

Postscript – the development of an environmental area in the school grounds

Between 1993 and 1995 the teacher instigated and developed a nature area within the school grounds. This was an area 20 metres by 10 metres which she transformed from a grass patch with three or four trees to a rich resource. It contained mown and unmown areas, a wood pile, a pond, a rocky mound, the original trees with other boundary trees added, and paths covered in wood bark which allowed access to the different parts with minimum disturbance to the habitats. It provided the one green area in this otherwise harsh asphalt environment, overshadowed by West Ham football stadium.

Figure 3.7 Charts summarizing the teaching and assessment of the topic

1st stage: planning	1st stage: assessment
Teaching/learning/assessing objectives	*Knowledge/concepts*
• assess children's observational skills	• parks: a place where there are things to play on
• listen to children's ideas conceprning the topic	• woods: unable to be distinguished from 'would'
• listen to what children would like to learn about	• wastelands: a place where people dump rubbish.
• encourage them to ask questions about the topic and note them down	*Observation* revolved around specific objects, i.e. things to play on in the park, piles of rubbish that they are told not to go near.
• listen to strands that could lead to investigations.	
	Initial questions about play equipment led to maths investigations. Also, what sort of rubbish?
Resources/events	
• display pictures of forest, trees, woodland, mammals and minibeasts;	*Previous experience:* Nobody had visited a wood or forest.
• show children's reference books;	
• put out collection of pooters, magnifying glasses, hand lenses, trays, dishes, pots.	
(to be changed regularly, throughout topic, with the children's work)	

Figure 3.7 cont.

2nd stage: planning

Teaching/learning/assessing objective

• use observation skills while visiting a park.

Activities planned

• share objective via story of Professor Sense
• draw Professor Sense
• visit local park for sensory visit
• revisit local park to draw a map of it
• listen to strands that could lead to investigative work.

2nd stage: assessment

Knowledge/concepts

• awareness of five senses (from Professor Sense story)
• there is more than one type of grass
• parks have flower beds, grass, bush areas as well as play areas.

Observations (sitting on the grass, remembering Professor Sense)

• scratching backs of legs
• little bits joined at the bottom
• waving greenness
• flower beds, grass, bushes, paths, play areas (mapping and visit).

(observations in park taped/added to as topic progressed)

Questions generated

• is all grass the same?
• how can we find out?
• does grass get into books, Miss?

Figure 3.7 cont.

3rd stage: planning	3rd stage: assessment
Teaching/learning/assessing objectives	*Asking questions*
• extend children's observational skills • develop questioning skills • explore possibilities within questions • listen for hypotheses in order to develop them • introduce idea of classification of animals • look in detail at one minibeast • develop their understanding of life cycle • look at wasteland opposite school – list contents and classify as helpful/harmful.	• all keen to ask questions; 29 generated after few days • basic questions from group A (oral) and B (written and oral); more specific ones from group C. *Classification of questions* • To Find Out: we can watch; read; investigate • accepting more than one way of doing things • generating questions from others' ideas • some questions could not be answered by class • hypotheses emerging.
Activities planned	*Answering* one question from each type; *planning* how to answer
• share objective – story and drawing of Professor Question • collect questions; classify questions (classification negotiated with children); answer questions • describe/share descriptions of minibeasts • make a database from descriptions • introduction to classification • classification games.	*Deepening observational skills* • drawing minibeast; writing five facts; sharing observations • understand need to use same characteristics for database *Knowledge/concept* • life cycle of their minibeast (reference books) • classification of animals (need for classification games to understand this).

Figure 3.7 cont.

4th stage: planning	4th stage: assessment
Teaching/learning/assessing objectives	*Five investigations* (each group did three)
• use questions decided on by children to develop observation and question skills, knowledge, research and investigative skills • develop hypotheses offered – discuss in light of further investigation and research • assess ability to plan an investigation • assess their awareness of fair testing • assess the means that they use to measure, record, interpret and communicate their findings • assess any ability to evaluate or reflect on their work and communicate their findings.	• where do worms like to live? • what makes a good home for an ant? • what lives in a tree? • what flowers do bees like best? • what leaves do aphids like to eat most? Detail from 'Where do worms like to live?' • three areas chosen: soil; grass; bushes by car park • taught – how to get worms out of the ground • pupils from groups A and B (slower learners) explained the task to next group It was noted that children: • found method of writing plans systematically • grew in independence of thought and action • hypothesized giving increasing detail and reasons • recognized more easily when they were not answering their original questions • became more confident about methods of recording • were more able to evaluate methods of working and confident to report if work did not go well.

Figure 3.7 cont.

5th and final stage: planning	5th and final stage: assessment
Teaching/learning/assessing objectives	*Visit to Epping Forest*
Assess the children's ability to plan an investigation that they want to carry out in Epping Forest	• it rained so data sheets had to be put away on the coach and children 'went on an adventure'
During the day	• fascinated by fungi, especially on fallen trees – and asked lots of questions
• assess the children's observational skills	• enjoyed the atmosphere and often stood and listened and watched quietly
• assess their ability to carry out their investigations.	• saw lots of animals – fox, squirrel, innumerable frogs
After the visit	• did some investigations but had to remember data – acknowledged this inaccuracy in their written accounts.
• assess their ability to display their findings	'I think I found more worms because there was good soil for them, plenty of places to hide from their enemies, and not many people walked there so they did not get squashed much.'
• assess their interpretations	
• assess their ability to communicate and to evaluate their work.	

4

Rabbit's House

YEARS 1 AND 2 (5 AND 6-YEAR-OLDS)

This chapter provides a window on a small piece of science teaching which was spread over only two weeks, and which comprises essentially one investigation. I have attempted to capture the way in which the teacher progressively focused the children's investigation, from an early exploration stimulated by a story to an investigation in which children could acquire good quality data. The teacher's attention to the thinking as well as the doing involved in the task, and her organization of successive groups in the class working on the investigation are documented.

The class was a Years 1 and 2 class (most of the children were 6 years old) in a school in Hackney in north London. The teacher shared with myself and a colleague several pieces of work, three of which are shown in Figures 4.1–4.3, and I pressed her to explain her accompanying teaching. For reasons which I have mentioned before, i.e. the almost intuitive 'unconscious' nature of teaching for an experienced teacher, I had to probe for what she regarded as obvious detail not worth mentioning. From this I built up an account which now forms this chapter and which is summarized

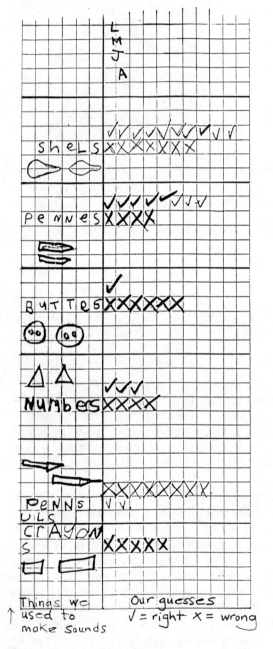

We were trying to guess the sounds in Rabbit's House :

Figure 4.1 Recording chart from group 4

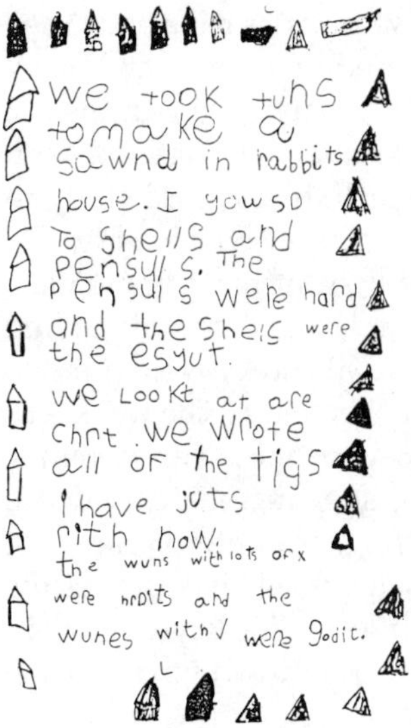

we took tuhs
to make a
sawnd in rabbits
house. I yowso
To shells and
pensuls. The
pensuls were hard
and the sheis were
the esyut.
we Lookt at are
chrnt. we wrote
all of the tigs
I have juts
rith how.
the wuns with lots of x
were hrduts and the
wunes with √ were goodit.

We took turns to make a sound in Rabbit's House.
I used two shells and pencils. The pencils were
hard and the shells were the easiest. We looked at
our chart. We wrote all of the things I have just
written now. The ones with lots of X were hardest
and the ones with √ were goodest.
L

Figure 4.2 Written account and drawing from L in Group 4

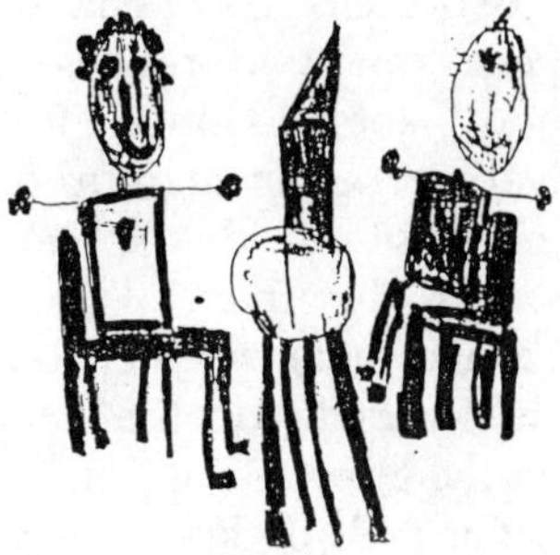

Wo are doeg
rabbits house
Ifgsd ot
the psno.
wdp the
ecst.
A

We are doing Rabbit's House. I
found out the pencils were the
easiest.
A

Figure 4.3 Written account and drawing from A in Group 4

in Figures 4.4 and 4.5. The account and summaries have been used in my teaching, in both pre-service and inservice courses, and many teachers have found they have enabled them to gain an insight into the implementation of exploration and investigation with young children; hence the decision to include this case study in the book. As with other chapters the first draft was read by the teacher and amendments made in the light of her comments.

The quality of the pieces of work and of the accompanying table was what first attracted my attention, and provoked me to find out about the teaching which had generated it. The work was from relatively young children (5 and 6-year-olds). The accounts, like the two shown were well set out, showing some evidence of chronological writing, factual reporting, and interpretation of data (Figures 4.2 and 4.3). The table (Figure 4.1) has the results clearly presented with proper labels, titles and a key to explain the significance of the ticks and crosses. The drawings show the experimental set-up within the classroom.

Even from just the two accounts, drawings and the table it is almost possible to piece together the details of the investigation. The children were investigating how easy it was to identify the sounds made by different objects. They had six pairs of objects – two shells, two pens, two buttons, two plastic numbers, two pencils and two crayons – and a large box which had been made into 'Rabbit's House'. The two children whose work is shown had worked in a group of four; one child was the subject who had to sit outside the house and try to identify the source of the sound. The other children selected one of the pairs of objects and banged them together to make a sound inside the house. If the child outside identified the source correctly a tick was recorded on the table and if not, a cross was recorded.

The table of data (Figure 4.1) was the element of the children's work which fascinated me most initially. It has all the features of a good table in that it conveys most of the information about the investigation. It has a title showing what the results refer to; the key explains what the symbols mean; and it is set out so that initial interpretation is relatively easy. We can, for instance, see that the noises from the shells and pens were identified more often than not; and that the noises from pencils, buttons and crayons were not easily recognized. The fact that it is drawn on squared paper means that if the results were inserted as the children were doing the experiment, they could keep track of what they had done, and see the pattern of data as it emerged. The original table was on a sheet of A1 size, clipped to a painting easel, so that the children could easily fill it in. It also had the advantage that others nearby could notice the results as they emerged, and it was also large enough for the teacher to hold up for a class discussion.

The drawings (Figures 4.2 and 4.3) show that the children were organized round a table, with the house on top of the table. The child listening to the sounds is on one side, and from the drawings we can see that this person had his/her back to the house. The chart is large and on a flipchart stand, as shown in L's drawing. L shows the sound 'clcl' being made on one side of the house.

Before looking at the children's writing which contains their interpretation of the results, it is worth examining the data to see what sense can be made of it. The shells were used in the investigation more times than any of the other objects (17 times) and the crayons were used the least (five times). It was not very easy to identify the sounds – there is no case where the sound was identified correctly right the way through. The proportion of number of times that the objects were guessed correctly could be regarded as giving an indication of how easy they were to identify. The objects come out in the order: pens; shells; numbers; pencils; buttons and crayons (67, 59, 43, 20, 14, 0 per cent, respectively). Obviously the idea of proportion will not be accessible to children of this age; it is more likely that they will spot where there are more ticks than crosses or the other way round, and that they will notice where there are lots of ticks and lots of crosses. Hence the shells rather than the pens may be identified as the best, and the pencils rather than the crayons as most difficult.

In turning to the children's writing we find that L (Figure 4.2) reported that 'the pencils were hard and the shells were the easiest'. Another child from the same group reported at the more general level 'that it was quite difficult to guess the noises'. Other children reported that the shells and pens were easy and the pencils were hard. A reports 'I found the pencil was the easiest'. This may in fact be true in that this could be a report of his personal finding (i.e. he himself found the pencils easiest and got them 'right') rather than an interpretation of the total evidence. The fact that none of the children mentioned the crayons and that the crayons were not used much may indicate that they were not that interested in them and forgot about them. Perhaps the rather dull sound of wax crayons contributed to the lack of interest.

One child explained how her interpretation fits the data by the use of the word 'because', stating that 'the pencils are hard to do *because* the pencils had more crosses and the pens is easy *because* they had more ticks'. The change in handwriting in Figure 4.2 indicates that L added her explanation, 'The ones with lots of x were hardest and the one with √ were goodest', at a later stage, possibly in response to the teacher asking 'How did you know?', or to class discussion of what was found.

Several children mentioned 'taking turns'. Cooperation had been a key learning intention on the part of the teacher (alongside data recording and interpretation). The reason for repetition in science is only slowly understood (see Chapter 2) and one child's comment, 'we got it right, so I did not go to have a go again', indicates limited understanding at this stage.

Examples of the children's work clearly showed their different stages of development. The task, in the way it was organized and supported, had allowed for differentiation in the outcome. The drawing and writing does not, however, show how the children organized themselves. A, in fact, played a key role in organizing the group, which emphasizes the importance of different methods of assessment to give a whole picture of a child. L, on the other hand, whose work is shown in Figure 4.2, giggled most of the way through the investigation because there happened to be someone making a video of the classroom that day, and in her case the written record revealed far more than the teacher's informal observations!

Given these features I asked the teacher for detail of the sequence of teaching, to explain how she had introduced the investigation, why it was called 'Rabbit's House', and how she had enabled relatively young children to produce and record data of considerable quality.

The investigation had started with a Masai story about Rabbit's House (Verna Aardema (1978) *Who's in Rabbit's House?*) in which Rabbit goes away from his house and when he returns he finds someone in his house: 'And a big bad voice from inside the house roared, "I am the Long One. I eat trees and trample on elephants. Go away! Or I will trample on you!"' Rabbit is frightened and does not know what to do; slowly one animal after another (Jackal, Leopard, Elephant, Rhinoceros) comes to the house and each time the same thing happens; they offer to use their strength in various ways to get the Long One out but all would involve the demolition

STORY	Who's in Rabbit's House (Masai story)
QUESTIONS	Could we recognize each other's voices? Could we deceive each other?
DISCUSSION	Generated ideas and strategies e.g. standing behind the screen, hands in front of face, listening on other side of the door
EXPLORATION	Tried out ideas informally – found that it was difficult to tell Let's try to investigate Rabbit's House – two children offer to make the house

IDENTIFY A FOCUSED PROBLEM	Problem What noises are easy to identify? How shall we do the investigation?
DISCUSSION	What could you use to make the noises? Should we have many things? How will you organize the activity? What shall we record? How shall we record? Suppose we start, what are the difficulties we are likely to meet?
SKELETON PLAN	Skeleton plan – list of objects to be used Hit two together to make a sound Record in chart like this
REMINDERS TO FIRST GROUP	Remember to make a prediction . . . decide which ones will be easiest to identify Remember to sort out about taking turns

Figure 4.4 Summaries of the first two class discussions

of Rabbit's House, which Rabbit forbids. Eventually the frog, who has been offering to help from the start, is eventually allowed to try. 'Frog said "I am the spitting cobra! I can blind you with my poison! Now come out of that house, or I'll squeeze under the door and spit poison into your eyes."' At which point a small caterpillar comes out of the house and Rabbit is able to enter.

The initial discussion of the story focused on what makes us afraid, but the teacher followed on by raising the questions of whether it was possible to recognize someone's voice if the person speaking could not be seen and whether it was possible for people to disguise their voices so that someone who knew them well could not identify them. This was one of the crucial points of the teaching. The two questions were drawn directly from the

Week 1	Story and early investigation Rabbit's House is made	whole class 1 two pupils
Week 2 Day 1	Whole class discuss design of the investigations Group 1 do investigation (two hours)	whole class 2 group 1
Day 2	Group 1 show data to class Whole class discuss communication and decide results would be better on squared paper and with labels Group 1 transcribe results to squared paper Group 2 undertake investigation (a.m.) using squared paper Group 3 undertake investigation (p.m.) using squared paper	whole class 3 group 1 group 2 group 3
Days 3 and 4	Groups 3, 4 and 5 undertake the investigation with no further help Groups 1, 2 and 3 write about what they had done	groups 3, 4, 5 groups 1, 2, 3
Day 5	Writing and drawings completed for all groups	
Start of week 3	Discussion of findings Shared writing for a class book	whole class 4

Figure 4.5   Summary of organization of teaching over two weeks

shared experience of the story, and were within the understanding of the children. The class were intrigued by them; some children offered ideas from their previous experience, while others were prepared to admit that they were not sure. The teacher quietly slipped in the question 'What could we do to find out?'

The children suggested that someone could go behind a screen or outside the door so that he/she could not see who was speaking and then try to identify the speaker in the class. They also suggested putting hands in front of the face to disguise the voice of the speaker. These were tried informally, and in some cases they did find it difficult to identify the speaker, but the class as a whole was not sure that there was conclusive evidence, so further investigation was necessary. The discussion ended with a decision to explore Rabbit's House more carefully, and two girls offered to make the house out of a cardboard box.

The reading of the story, the subsequent discussion and the informal trying of the experiment all took place with the class sitting as a group 'on the carpet' with the teacher as discussion leader, and it took about an hour.

When the house was made, the teacher again set aside time to discuss the planning of the investigation with the whole class. The first task was to focus the problem and to decide how to go about finding an answer to it. The question selected, 'What sounds are easy to identify?', is relatively straightforward and very close to the question used in the first informal exploration the previous week. This was important because the investigation the children eventually undertook was a refinement of a 'practice run'. The children were able to suggest that they would have to make different noises and that someone who was not watching would try and guess what made the noise.

With older children it might be possible to leave them at this point to design the investigation but younger children need considerable support. Like other teachers quoted in this book, this teacher aims to give children sufficient guidance to enable them to get started, but to leave some parts slightly open ended, so that the children have to address the problems as they come to them.

In this case she questioned them about methods of making noises, equipment that could be used ('What could you use to make the noises?' 'Should we have many things?'), organization ('How will you organize the activity?'), what to record ('What shall we record?'), and how to record ('How shall we record?'). In her teaching, she was not telling the children what to do, but helping to identify for them the things they needed to think about so that they had to make the decisions themselves. More importantly she expected children to listen to and evaluate each other's suggestions.

After some time a skeleton plan emerged to which the whole class had subscribed. The children were to use six pairs of classroom objects to hit together and they would record their findings on a chart. (Figure 4.6 shows this chart, as it was completed by the first group). The objects would be hidden in the house and one person would be outside listening, with another person choosing which pair of objects to use for the sound. Crosses would be used to record wrong identification and ticks, correct identification. They would work in groups.

When most of the important decisions were made she used the question 'Suppose we start, what are the difficulties we are likely to meet?' She used this often to give an opportunity for last-minute thoughts and questions about procedures, and to make the children think ahead.

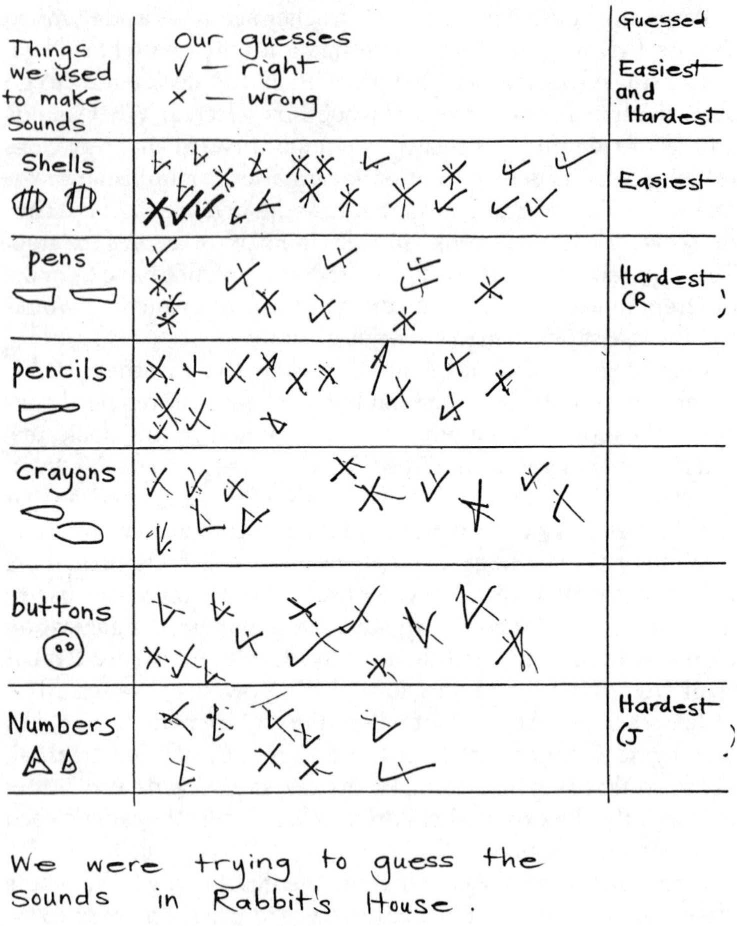

Things we used to make Sounds	Our guesses ✓ — right ✗ — wrong	Guessed Easiest and Hardest
Shells		Easiest
pens		Hardest (CR)
pencils		
crayons		
buttons		
Numbers		Hardest (J)

We were trying to guess the sounds in Rabbit's House.

Figure 4.6   Initial recording chart from group 1

The first group to start work on the investigation was given extra advice in the form of further things to think about and do: 'Remember to make a prediction – you have to decide first which ones you think will be easiest to identify' and 'Remember to sort out about taking turns.' This first group worked for about two hours and produced a chart with lots of ticks and crosses.

The record of the data from the first group displayed on the chart was shown to the whole class at the start of the next day.

The teacher asked the other children to look at the results and decide what it told them. Questions about the meaning of the ticks and crosses led naturally to the idea that it is useful to add explanation by means of a key. The children also found that trying to make sense of the numbers of ticks and crosses turned out to be tedious because they were jumbled up. 'What could we do about it?' The suggestion that squared paper would be better emerged; with the ticks on one line – one per box – and the crosses on the adjoining line. This process of identifying and sharing a problem with the whole class and requiring the children to sort it out is an important strategy. The improved method of recording on squared paper was used by all subsequent groups. This little episode gives an example of one of the loose ends which had been left from the initial planning, and which was used very productively as part of the teaching.

The leaving of this loose end was not an accident. The teacher deliberately chose to do this, knowing that it would raise issues about ways of recording, and about the ways that facilitate interpretation of results. She attaches a high importance to allowing children to make mistakes and learn from them. She explained further that it was part of 'the process of learning *why* we use particular forms of charts or tables, rather than just seeing tables as a convention'.

Before looking at the subsequent set of events, it is worth noting that by this point there had been three substantial elements of whole-class teaching which had taken place. The first one focused on trying out an early exploration; the second developed the exploration into a more systematic investigation with detailed plans for procedure; the third evaluated and improved the method of recording. What can be seen in action and in context here is the explicit teaching of the different stages of an investigation.

The third discussion also helped to remind subsequent groups about what they had to do when it was their turn to collect data, so that group 2 took over the equipment and did the investigation with little further help from the teacher. At the same time group 1 transferred their data on to the new form of chart and realized as they were doing it that a pattern was emerging that they could see quite easily. The first and second charts of group 1 are shown in Figures 4.6 and 4.7 respectively. This reorganizing of the chart is reported in the writing of one of the children in group 1:

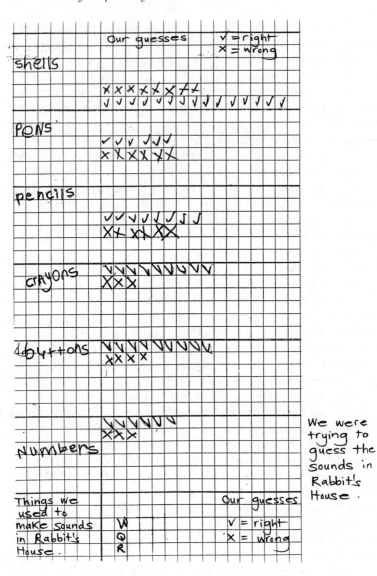

Figure 4.7 Final recording chart from group 1

People couldn't see how many ticks and crosses there was, so we had to do another one. We had to do them in a straight line.

A fuller description and explanation is given in the class book on the project which is put together jointly by the teacher and the children. The captions accompanying the charts in the book are:

This is the first chart we made. It was hard to see what we had found out so we did another one.

When we made a new chart we marked off each tick and cross as we did it on the new chart so that we did not get in a muddle.

This is the second chart we made. We decided the squared paper would help us to make partners of the ticks and crosses and see if there were more ticks or crosses.

There were five groups in the class successively undertaking the investigation and then drawing pictures and writing about it; the sequence of work is shown in Figure 4.5. The groups were not of even size: groups 1 and 2 comprised three children each, group 3 eight (which split into two for carrying out the investigation, hence their spanning two days for the investigation, but all data was put on the same chart), group 4 had four children (this is the group whose work is shown in Figures 4.1, 4.2 and 4.3), and group 5 nine (again this group divided as group 3 had done). Obviously while children were not working on some aspect of Rabbit's House they were engaged on other learning activities. (See Chapter 7 for one teacher's mechanisms for organizing several tasks in one classroom.)

The teacher now moved to the last of the whole-class discussions, which reviewed everybody's findings and brought ideas together for the 'class book', which is literally a book the whole class make together with the teacher and which records the work from a particular study (more details of it are given below). The focus of this discussion was the tables of data – all of them, including the first one which had been modified. This latter point is important; children will easily dismiss early attempts which they regard as 'wrong', and yet it is in the process of improvement that some of the best thinking is done. Unless the teacher shows children how to value these early attempts as an intrinsic and essential part of learning, an important contribution to the children's growing confidence will be lost. The extracts from the class book given above concerning the charts were written by the teacher from what the children in the first group told her. Questions such as 'What was the problem with the first chart?' 'How did you make sure you did not get in a muddle when you went from one chart to the other?' 'Why did you use squared paper?' 'How did it help?' will evoke such responses.

The teacher explained: 'The purpose of this was also to compare the findings across the whole class, using the charts to see if any general patterns could be seen. I asked them to look for similarities and differences between the charts, rather than just recounting their experiences and memories of what they did and found out.'

The role model of the teacher in reviewing what has been learnt is an important part of this last phase of the teaching. It values the thinking as well as the doing of the investigation. This is the summary found at the end of the class book:

We talked about the What's in Rabbit's House? game:

1 We thought we should do each sound a number of times. Most of us did the shells the most.
  Christopher thinks we kept on doing shells because we liked getting it right.
2 We noticed if we did the game for a long time we got good at it.
3 Most people found the shells were the easiest.
4 Some people found the bricks were the easiest.
5 Some people thought the buttons sounded like the shells.

The production of the class book is also part of the teaching. It shows how books are put together; it has a front cover with a title and author on it (*What's in Rabbit's House?* by Orange Class) and an illustration, one of the children's pictures. The front cover is made slightly larger than the inside pages; it has the spine strengthened and is covered in tacky-back to keep it clean, as it will be handled by many readers.

Inside is the introductory page on which is written: 'We made sounds in Rabbit's House and tried to guess what they were. We drew pictures, did some writing and made some charts to show what we did and what we discovered.' Then we find the charts, drawings and writing from each successive group. The chart first and then each child has typically a two-page spread – the writing is on the right, with the drawing and the typed version of the writing on the left. None of the children's writing has corrections on it; the teacher merely asked the children to read out the writing to her and she typed it out with adult spelling on the computer. She uses their own writing diagnostically to decide what is the next area to develop for that particular child.

One of the charts was drawn by the children themselves, which was noted as part of the story: 'E, V and J made this chart all by themselves. They decided to use the bricks as well.' One child's writing shows another little decision that had to be made in carrying out this investigation: 'if they guess it wrong they can't have another guess'. There is more evidence of interpretation in the form of seeing a pattern in data: 'We got more ticks than crosses for everything.' There is evidence of willingness to share predictions and findings even if they were different, and to give a reason for why some sounds were hard to identify: 'When I was playing in Rabbit's House, I thought the bricks were the easiest but they weren't. The shells were the easiest. When it was my turn I did a hard one, the bricks. The bricks sounded like the pencils so the bricks were hard.'

The class book ends up as a 64-page book – with a beginning, middle and end. The work of all the 27 children in the class is included. It holds, in an attractive and robust form, much of the children's thinking alongside their work, for perusal later. Class books were made for all topics and they became some of the most popular reading books for the children, either on their own or in groups of two or three, who could often be found discussing aspects of their previous work as they read through the books together.

Before closing this chapter, I am including a few comments about helping young children to participate in discussion, and about the organization of this teacher's classroom.

Sustaining whole-class discussions for up to an hour with young children is not achieved without explicit teaching and practice. This teacher gave the children specific training to help them to recognize the importance of listening and of allowing someone to finish speaking; she had an object (it happened in her class to be a large conch shell) that was passed to the speaker; the child holding the shell was allowed to speak; others who did not hold it had to listen. Her own actions and responses were also important because of the role model which teachers provide for their pupils. She had to listen carefully and to give careful consideration to what each child said. Her use of questions to extend their thinking, many examples of which are in the text, is part of the key to her success – 'Can you tell us a bit more about that?' 'How did you do this?' 'What shall we do about this problem?'

Good classroom organization is crucial. In this teacher's classroom, the position of resources are carefully organized and maintained, so that children know where things are and little time is wasted on giving out equipment and resources. Daily routines, carried out by the children for maintaining and checking resources, play an important role in helping children to take responsibility and to feel a sense of ownership and pride in the environment. Above all it releases the teacher for more important interactions with the children.

5

Ourselves

YEAR 2 (6 AND 7-YEAR-OLDS)

This case study comes from a school in west London. The design of the displays, making the classroom look like a well-organized 'Aladdin's cave' full of treasures, first caught my eye and prompted my request to the teacher to include her work. The Pine class scientist (Figure 5.1) epitomizes the activities in which the children were engaged. (Classes in this school are named after trees, hence the 'Pine'.) I found examples of observational and illustrative practical work as well as an investigation; measurement leading to data collection; data interpretation; use of information books and videos to find information to support first-hand findings; systematic research to solve a real problem; and the involvement of the local community in the topic.

The material for the chapter was collected by photographing (towards the end of the topic) the classroom and the adjoining sections of the corridor, by talking with the teacher, by studying children's work, by examining the teacher's written records and by the teacher reading and amending an early draft of the chapter.

The topic of Ourselves was taught from the beginning of January

Figure 5.1 The Pine class scientist

to half-term in February, i.e. about six weeks. It took up most of the time, each and every day, for those six weeks so it had to carry nearly all areas of the curriculum. Some cross-curricular aspects are apparent in the description that follows, but by focusing on the science much of the detail of other subjects has not been included.

Within the area of Living things, which was the topic specified in the school's planning grid, the focus of Ourselves and the even narrower foci of What are the parts inside our bodies? and What do they do?, as well as The needs of living things, were selected by the teacher for the study. The children had previously studied Ourselves in the reception class (4 to 5-year-olds), but had focused on external features and senses. More recent work had covered minibeasts and growth in plants, and it was this that had partly determined the focus on human beings as examples of living things. The teacher was not sure at the start how much she would cover in the time, but in the event, the needs of living things, the skeleton, the respiratory system, the heart, the brain were included, as well as the idea of diversity within human beings (height, shoe size, skin colour) and growth and change. Of these, the brain was not something which the teacher had envisaged teaching; its inclusion was instigated by the children.

A lively feature of the classroom was the Pine class busy body – a life-size cut-out which hung from the ceiling of the classroom and acted as a summary of the work covered. Each new part of the body learnt about was added in words on one side of the figure; on the reverse side were drawings of the parts of the body, added systematically as the topic progressed. By the end, cut-outs of heart, ribs, lungs and windpipe had been attached at appropriate places; the brain had been stuck on; bones, muscles and blood vessels had been drawn in. The words written on the body were used in an adaptation of the song 'I have a busy body, a very busy body, and it goes everywhere with me. And on that body, I've got a . . .', with verses such as 'I've got a body, a very busy body, and it goes everywhere with me. And in that body, I've got a heart, and it goes everywhere with me. With a bump thump here, bump, thump there, bump, thump, bump, thump everywhere . . . , goes everywhere with me . . .'

In addition to the knowledge about the human body, the teacher was keen to develop further the children's skills in measuring, which had been the focus of the mathematics work in the previous term, and to teach them about using tables and presenting data in an organized way. The topic easily provided opportunities for this as can be seen in the work described later in the chapter.

The children were not particularly excited by the topic at first as they thought they knew all about their bodies, but it was not long before they realized there was a lot more to learn and they became engrossed. There were also two model skeletons that had been put up in the classroom, one of which showed not only the bones but many of the organs in the body. To begin with the children gave them at most a cursory glance, and in some cases appeared to find them distasteful, but before long they were going to them and having very serious discussions about what all the parts were and how many bones they had.

Hair

One of the key events in getting the children more involved and interested was the studies and investigation on hair. There was a sudden awakening of interest when the children realized that they could do investigations on themselves. While not the first activity, it was done very early in the topic.

Early descriptive work where children sought words to describe hair was followed by an investigation of hair strength. It was an investigation which lent itself to the use of a table for recording the results (Figure 5.2) and hence reinforced understanding of the use of tables. It is, in fact, an investigation which can be used for a variety of materials (hair, threads of wool, cotton, etc.) and variants of it can be found in other books. Given the relatively low weights needed to be hung on the bottom of hair before it snaps, the use of paper clips is sensible and is simple to resource.

Interpretation is less easy. Children have a tendency to isolate a single factor as significant (long, curly), e.g. 'long hair is stronger than short hair' but several children quickly realized that more than one factor was coming into play.

Having got the class interested, what else was done? In outline, one system of the body after another was studied. Each new system was started by a discussion or other exercise which enabled the teacher to find out what the class knew already. She then tended to give them activities they could engage in together in small groups, but as children finished activities at different times,

Whose hair?	Colour	Length	number of paper clips
J	black	33 cm	122
J	blonde	16 cm	72
S	red	16 cm	29

Figure 5.2 Table of data on hair

their studies diverged. The considerable use of secondary sources of information meant that children could easily work by themselves at different rates. Sometimes a child might read 'ahead' about the next system of the body to be studied, or, as was the case in the study of the brain, a small interest group, often led by the more able children, would choose to explore something on their own, but with the teacher's permission.

Monitoring overall learning

Day-to-day activities provide teachers with information about the children's learning, and one or two of the incidents that this teacher selected as examples of significant learning are included in the section on learning activities later in this chapter. In this section I have included four activities which were planned specifically to help the teacher elicit information about what the children knew and could do. The first is a brainstorming exercise used at the start. The second is a problem-solving exercise, which required the children to use a range of knowledge and skills which were being developed. The third was a drawing task done individually by all the children both before and after teaching to see the difference. The fourth was an exercise in interpreting data which was done systematically with each child and required individual interviews.

Initial brainstorming – living things

Children were asked at the start to write down their definitions of living things and then, working in groups of four or five, to sort pictures into two sets: living and non-living. Most of the class had no difficulty in doing this, but there were a few children who classified televisions and motor bikes as living because they moved. This is not at all unusual and confirms findings from research (Osborne and Freyberg 1985). The teacher used the children's definitions and their grouping to draw out from a group discussion as many things as possible that living things do. The list covered mainly eating, breathing, growing, and moving. These four ideas were therefore developed alongside the work on the structure of the body. The subject of reproduction tends to be difficult at this age as children cannot relate it to themselves, so this was not included.

Setting a problem to use and develop knowledge of the needs of living things

The teacher wanted the children to think quite seriously about the needs of living things to help them to understand the significance of the functions of the parts of the body. She wanted them to understand for instance that we have mechanisms for getting air and food into the body, because the body needs air and food. The idea of needs, however, has to extend to the environment in which something lives (the need for appropriate temperature, safety, shelter, etc.) as well as focusing on the things that have to be taken into the body. The teacher decided at this point that children had a greater chance of understanding 'needs of living things' in relation to an animal that had to be looked after, rather than in relation to themselves; she therefore set the problem of choosing a pet for the classroom. This was not a simulated problem – they really were to buy and care for the chosen pet. By May the class had acquired two pet goldfish following careful research into the problem. An additional reason for choosing pets as opposed to humans was that the research which had to be done in order to decide what was the most appropriate pet required research in books; whereas if they had considered their own needs they would have drawn only on their experience. A constraint was the budget – a little over £20 from the class fund.

The four pets suggested initially by the children were goldfish, hamster, gerbil and parrot; there was no difficulty in recognizing that cats and dogs were unsuitable. The class decided in discussion with the teacher that they would have to find out about the cost of buying and maintaining the animal; the size of container it would need; the items to go inside the container; and features that made the animal interesting. The children also realized that there would probably not be one unique solution to the problem so a choice would have to be made. The choice was made eventually by every child voting. The original inclusion of a parrot in the list came from the story *The Pet Shop* in the Funny Bones series, in which the parrot in the shop keeps shouting out 'You've got a big bum' and the teacher is sure that they all think it would be very funny having such things shouted out in school.

Finding appropriate information books was not easy. They had to have pictures in them so that children who were not reading fluently could still find and extract considerable information. The Dorling Kindersley books on pets and the slightly old-fashioned Ladybird books proved some of the most useful; the researching in books worked well for all levels of children. The research extended to interviewing the ladies at the local pet shop, whose cooperation had been sought, and received, in advance by the teacher, to find out the price of each animal and the cost of feeding and bedding. It was this part of the research that revealed that parrots would cost about £500, and led to the substitution of a budgerigar for the parrot in the list. The trips were planned so that small groups would be taken to the shop by the support teacher who worked with the class on Tuesday mornings.

Figure 5.3 shows one of the four posters that were in the classroom with the results of the research, along with two of the poems written about buying a pet.

Once the voting had taken place (the goldfish 'won' by one vote), the two goldfish were finally bought for the start of the summer term. Setting up the rotas for their care and maintenance was incredibly valuable. The children were made to do this themselves; to make sure that everyone had a turn, but also that the fish were not overfed. Coping with weekends made them look at

Can I have a pet please?

Can I have a pet please?
A puppy or a mouse would be nice
Or I wouldn't mind a cat
Or a bird would be nice
Can I have a pet please?
A hamster?
O.K.
Let's go down to the pet shop
And buy one
Before you change your mind

Thomas and Kaja

Can I have a pet please?

Can I have a pet please?
Can we have a dog please?
A fish will do
We will clean its tank
We will feed it
We will love it everyday.

Lee and Sara

Figure 5.3 Display of information researched about a pet

dates carefully, and they had to make sure that the Friday feeders put in the pellets which will last two days.

Of the four activities selected for this section, this problem solving looks least like an assessment tool. Good assessment tools are usually good learning activities, so it is often not possible to distinguish them. The purpose to which they are put and the way they are used tend to determine their classification into one or other.

This example shows that children of this age can rise to the challenge of such a problem; they can collect and evaluate information on a problem that interests them; they can use a variety of sources for their information (books, pamphlets, people); they can (with help) ask appropriate questions to elicit the information they want; they can evaluate available resources to help them make choices (e.g. the eventual decision to take the much loved idea of a parrot off the list); they can come up with an answer in which the teacher has sufficient confidence to follow it through to the purchase of the pet.

Before moving to the third assessment tool, it is worth pausing to review the organization of this one. First there were four groups, each of which took on the responsibility of researching one of the animals and displaying the information for everyone. The teacher had a support teacher once a week. Originally all groups were to go to the pet shop but in the event the supply teacher was ill for some of the time and only one group went. One child from each of the pet groups was selected to take questions for the whole group. In every case the teacher selected a child for whom English was not their home language in order to boost their confidence. One of the important lessons to be learnt by the children from such an activity is that reliable information cannot be collected quickly; that often two or three sources need to be consulted because no single source has all the information needed; that it is possible to pick up conflicting information from two different sources, necessitating further research. Even the voting cannot be done at one instance in time. This problem was a shared problem: the care of the pet was to be shared, and therefore everyone had to be involved in the voting. The absence of one or two children through illness had to be allowed for by having a voting box in which children could put their votes. The opening of the box was then done only after everyone had had an opportunity to cast his/her vote.

The teacher had wondered if the children would vote for the

pet they had researched, but this did not necessarily happen; an indication that some really were evaluating the information sensibly and making an informed decision.

A minor interesting point was the naming of the fish as Rose and Lily; not two names that the teacher would have expected or chosen herself. She realized, however, that she had recently been talking to the class about a Victorian painting in which there were two little girls called Rose and Lily. Children sometimes make links the teacher does not anticipate!

In reflecting overall on how the children tackled this problem, she commented that 'their behaviour modelled adults'; they could pick up the problem at odd points, find out a few more points, record them and then go on with other activities. Their interest was maintained over several weeks.

What is inside our bodies – drawings before and after teaching

The third assessment tool was children's drawings. These provided the teacher with an indication of what the children knew about what was inside their bodies near the start of the topic (January), and what they knew by the end of the topic (February). The task comprised merely a request to the children to draw what was inside their bodies on to a template; it is similar to the tasks used in the SPACE project (see Chapter 2). The drawings shown in Figure 5.4 are typical of the sort of changes evident in many of the pictures. The number of parts drawn had increased; position was better understood; more labels were known; detail in the wrist and hand were shown on many drawings; the spine was present in several although it is difficult to tell whether spine or breast bone had been included if they are not labelled; the skull has specific sockets for the eye and ear. It is of course likely that the increase in knowledge is greater than that shown, because children are often able to tell you things which they do not put down on paper.

Compared with the problem-solving activity, this was easy to organize. All the class can do the drawing at the same time. Individual attention was needed for those children who had difficulty writing the labels; the teacher asked them what the parts were called and she then wrote in what the children told her.

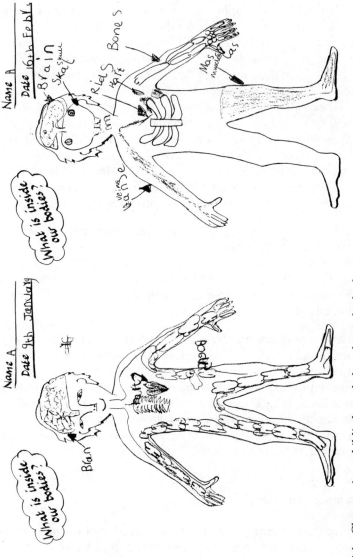

Figure 5.4 Changes in a child's knowledge about the body

Exercise in interpreting data

As mentioned earlier, one of the teacher's objectives was to help children be able to use evidence, especially evidence related to measurements and displayed in tables. Towards the end of the topic the teacher devised a task which would test the children's ability to extract and interpret information from a table. The task was similar to those devised by Goldsworthy and Feasey (1993) for helping children interpret data in tables and charts. In order to be successful the children had to be able to recall the sort of measurements that they had made of their own handspan, otherwise they would not have known that the data given was larger and therefore likely to belong to adults. The child's response shown in Figure 5.5 was typical of many of the answers and showed considerable ability on the part of the child in reading and using tables of data. Overall, all the children (25 of them) were able to answer the questions correctly except for:

- three children who could not recognize that the numbers referred to 'grown-ups';
- three who could not cope with such high numbers, but the teacher suspects they could work with smaller numbers;
- two who did not know how to use the data to help them answer the question.

Given the quite sophisticated skill needed to read rows and columns on tables and understand what is related to what, this is quite impressive for the age group.

The acquisition of an appropriate pet, the increase in knowledge about living things, the ability to interpret data and the realization that people can be the subject of an investigation were some of the outcomes of this topic. What were some of the other activities which led to these outcomes?

Learning activities

One of the interesting aspects of the collection of learning activities that this teacher devised, or selected from various sources, is their active nature. They used a vast amount of first-hand evidence, things that the children can observe and measure themselves, even though it is not possible to 'take the lid' off the body and

Name: ᴋ.

Handspan Data

Name	Hand Span	Arm Reach
Karalyn	17	69
Fred	18	67
Jenny	20	67
Malcolm	20	84
Anne	21	66
Vincent	22	73
Matt	23	78
Jo	24	76
Jack	24	77

How do you know these people are probably grown-ups?
    Cause they have big numbers

Do people with big hands have long arms?
    yes
    no

How do you know?
    Malcolm has got 20 and 84. Jack has got 24 and 77.
    So Malcolm has got smaller hands but bigger arms.

Figure 5.5 'Data probe' to gauge children's ability to read data

```
ID Card

Name

Address

DoB

                        I am            years old

My height                        _____      cm

My reach                         _____      cm

My handspan                      _____      cm

My stride                        _____      cm

My eye colour  _____

My hair        _____
```

Figure 5.6   Personal ID cards

have a look inside. Much of the information gained in this way, about the outside of the body and about what it can do, is used to link with the information about the inside gleaned from books and other secondary sources.

Data collection on themselves

Making the ID cards shown in Figure 5.6 was an important part of the topic. It did not in fact take long, as many of the measurements had been made the previous term in the work on measurement in mathematics, and further information needed such as the length of the spine was added with little difficulty because of the skills the children had. The box of ID cards was a database constantly referred to by the children. They could extract information about several children and put them on one table, they could use them to solve problems set by the teacher and to answer questions generated by themselves (see Figure 5.7, 'Does the person with the longest arms have the biggest handspan?').

Sometimes problems were generated between the children in

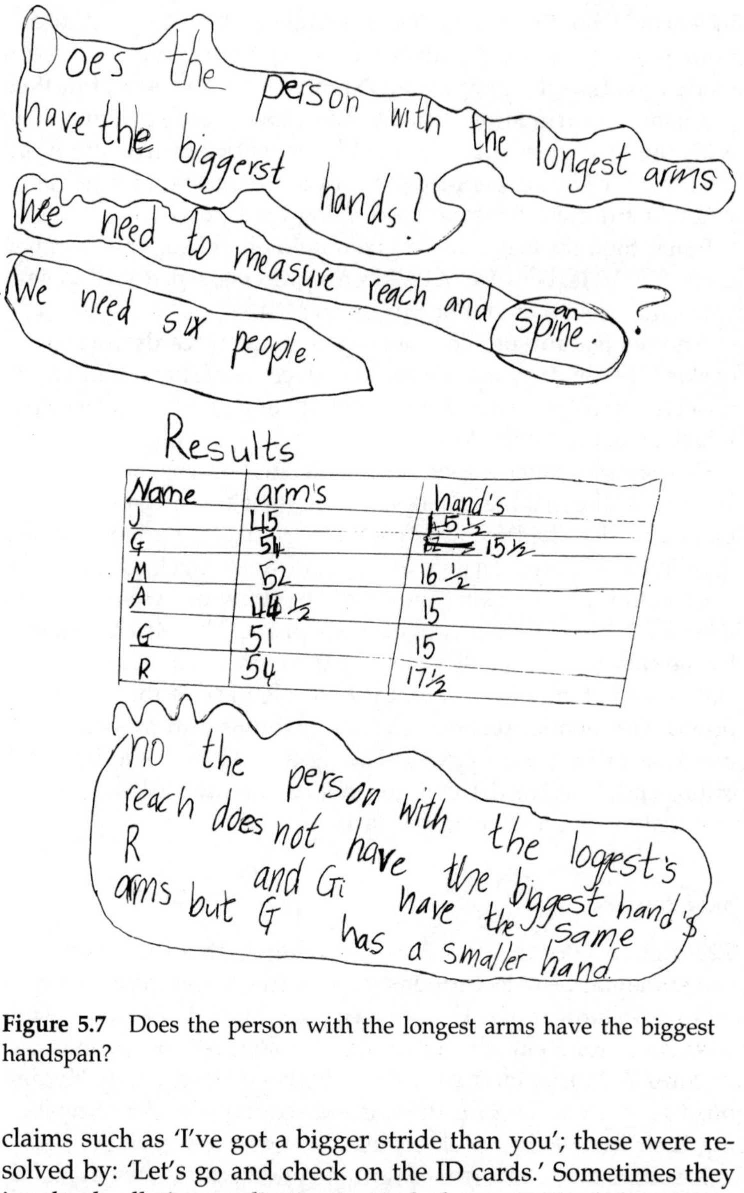

Does the person with the longest arms have the biggerst hands?

We need to measure reach and spine.?

We need six people.

Results

Name	arm's	hand's
J	45	15½
G	54	15½
M	52	16½
A	44½	15
G	51	15
R	54	17½

no the person with the longest's reach does not have the biggest hand's R and Gi have the biggest hand's arms but G has a smaller hand. same

Figure 5.7 Does the person with the longest arms have the biggest handspan?

claims such as 'I've got a bigger stride than you'; these were resolved by: 'Let's go and check on the ID cards.' Sometimes they involved collating qualitative instead of quantitative information, such as that needed to answer the question 'Do all black people have curly hair?'

It is important not to underestimate the practice that is needed in learning how to use tables. The teacher reported that at one point a group that were investigating handspan and arm reach made a table, with columns for Name, Hand and Arm, but then put hand and arm measurements randomly in each column. Even with the teacher's help they could not work out that the numbers were in the wrong place. It raised the question for her as to whether they should have been using a table.

Some thought needs to be given beforehand to what features go on ID cards, because of children's growing sensitivity. Weight was quite deliberately not put on the list.

Another feature studied, but not put on the ID cards, was colour of skin. The children investigated the diversity of skin colour within the classroom and experimented with mixing paint to find a colour which matched their skin tone.

One simple exercise associated with close observation of themselves was the making of face jigsaws. The children were put into pairs and they had to draw each other's faces, noting carefully distinctive features: shapes of eye and nose, freckles, colour of eyes, colour of hair, skin tones, etc. The drawings were made on a three by three grid with quite large squares. This was transferred by the children to a smaller three by three grid, so that they appreciated something of the way it is possible to scale things up and down. The smaller pictures were stuck on to card and cut up in order to make a face jigsaw. The jigsaws were made up quite often, and it made the children notice carefully the relation of one feature to another on the face.

Skeleton

Children, by the age of 7, know something about skeletons, because they appear in cartoons, stories (the Funny Bones series) and non-fiction books. In one sense they know they have a skeleton, but somehow do not make the connection between the pictures and cartoons and their own bodies. Consequently 'finding our bones' by feeling for them is a discovery – a sort of reviewing their knowledge of skeletons through a new perspective.

A simple fact is that bones cannot bend because they are hard; so if the body bends at any point there must be a joint between two bones. One activity therefore involved the children drawing round their hands putting a cross where a bend occurred, trying to work out how many bones they had in their hands and then referring to the books to check out how many of the total they had found. The sheer number of little bones that are present in the wrist (necessary to allow the complicated movements that our hands can make) is always a surprise to children, but of course these cannot all be felt from the outside. The fact that several of the drawings of the body at the end of the topic showed the many finger and wrist bones indicated that children had registered and remembered this (refer back, for instance, to the right-hand drawing in Figure 5.4).

Hunting the bends in their bodies to find the joints helped the children understand the significance of these for their movement. They made models of their arms and legs (cardboard for the bones, split pin paper clips for the joints), carefully counting the bends to get the models as accurate as possible.

Spine, ribs and skull were also easily found by feeling, and the length of the spine was added to the ID card. It is interesting to note that the brain in the February drawing in Figure 5.4 is shown outside the skull but inside the head, giving yet another example of what could be used as the basis of a conversation between the teacher and the child.

Hung in the classroom were three 'basic' skeletons made out of strips of thick paper to form 3D models. One was normal size, one half size and one twice normal size.

Heart

Many people cannot easily find their pulse, so the task set in the sheet shown in Figure 5.8 was not that straightforward. The children did, however, become aware of the beating of their hearts in PE, anticipating it partly because the teacher had talked to them about the effect of exercise on the heartbeat.

There was a lovely incident which occurred during PE. One child, who was not a particularly fast learner, suddenly rushed over and asked the teacher to feel his heart beating; it was going quickly because he was exercising. He knew this and was delighted to have noticed that what had been discussed in class applied to him. For him, this was a discovery.

PE reinforced the work on the body. The teacher had also found the information that 7-year-old children are able to run for ten minutes without stopping and had read this to the class, who were keen to try. She made the children build up to this slowly

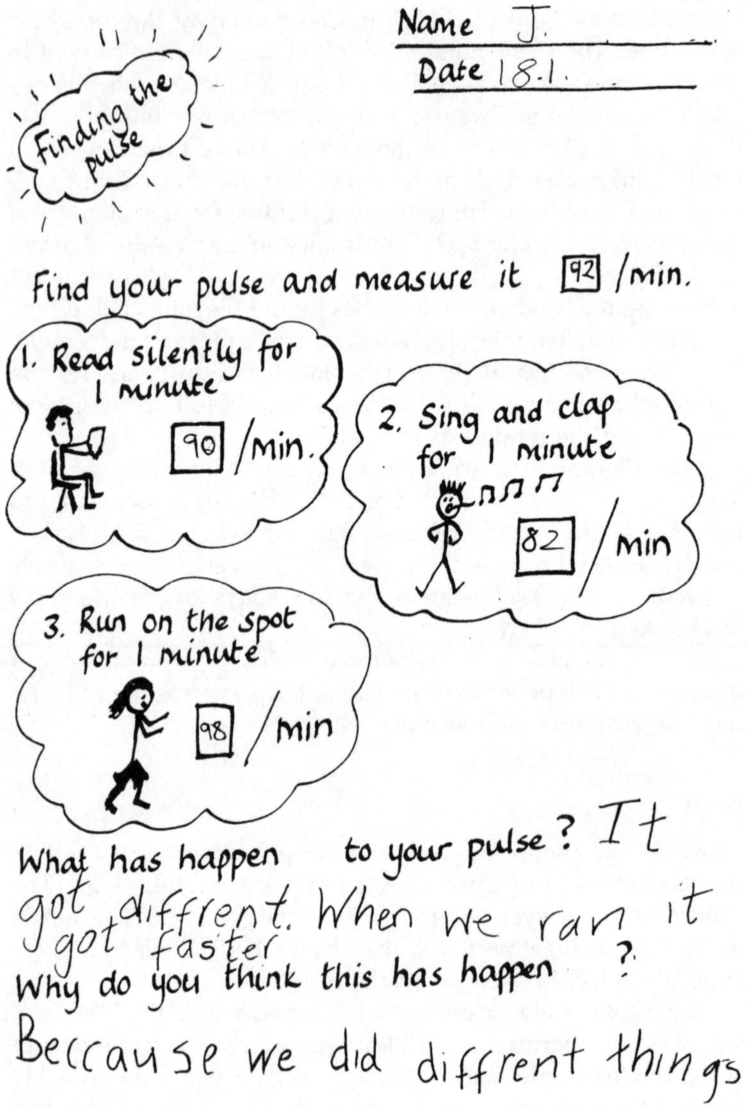

Figure 5.8 What happens to your pulse when you exercise?

– one minute, then two minutes with children being allowed to stop when they had had enough. Some got up to eight minutes and were pressing her to time them for ten minutes. Their legs felt like jelly and they could feel their hearts pounding.

Lungs – breathing

Learning about where the lungs are, how big they are and what they look like was done mainly through the teacher talking to the class, showing them pictures and allowing them to look up information in books. It was in this context that the teacher related an incident which had stuck in her mind:

> I had asked one child [of average ability] to look in information books and find out about lungs for the class 'busy body'. About a fortnight later when I was starting to talk about lungs to lead up to an investigation, the child put up his hand and described the lungs, where they are in the body, function, etc. This was significant because this child [not usually interested in science] had been inspired. He had read information about lungs, discussed it with his parents, etc. and had been able to remember it all.

So 'information told by the children' must be added to the list of how this section was taught.

The investigation referred to by the teacher was titled 'What happens when we breathe?' It moved from qualitative observations (What happens to the chest when we breathe?) to quantitative observations, involving both measurement and calculation, and finally to thinking about how that might relate to what is going on inside. As with the whole body, drawings were again used to find out what children knew about the parts of the body which help us to breathe.

Growth

Young children first think of growth only in terms of 'getting bigger', but they cannot readily answer 'how much bigger?'. Preparing the display shown in Figure 5.9 (drawing round a child and an adult) helped give the idea of the relative sizes.

The children brought in photographs they had of themselves when younger and built up their own personal timelines, showing

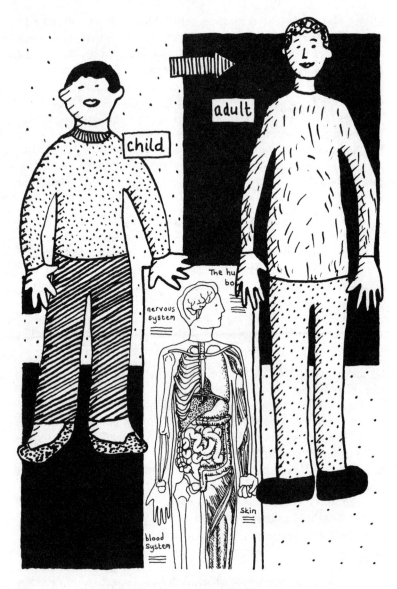

Figure 5.9 Growth: comparison of child with adult

how they had changed. Growth is much more than 'getting bigger' – this was a point the teacher brought out in her discussions with the children; she even related it back to the work which had been done on plants the previous term – as a plant grows it also does not just 'get bigger'. An appreciation of the increased skill and changing functions of themselves even in a fairly short lifetime is well appreciated by the child whose work is featured in Figure 5.10.

The mother of one of the children was expecting a baby and was having regular photographs taken from an echoscan; she was prepared to lend these to the teacher so that the children could see the growth. Normally the teacher found that the children had little interest in babies, but this time they were really interested to see the baby when it was born.

Senses

This was not a major part of the work, more like revision from a previous topic. The teacher used a story which was a spoof on Little Red Riding Hood and had appeared in *Guardian* Education (Baird 1994). She decided she could adapt it as a drama exercise for her class. (The original story had Grandma telling Little Red Riding Hood all about her big ears and what they could do etc. until eventually she had revised all her GCSE Biology for her!) So the children acted out a similar drama with the one playing Grandma telling Red Riding Hood about the senses, not to GCSE level but at their own level.

Brain

This study was mainly done by one independent small group. The teacher, however, did spend a little time talking with the class about the brain as the part of your body which sends messages to make the rest of the body work. To enable the class to appreciate the complexity of messages and incidentally to do a valuable language exercise, she got the children to give her messages (to her arm) in order to make it pick up a pencil. She only did exactly what they told her and they realized how difficult it was to give precise instructions! Through playing the game several times their ability to express their ideas improved no end.

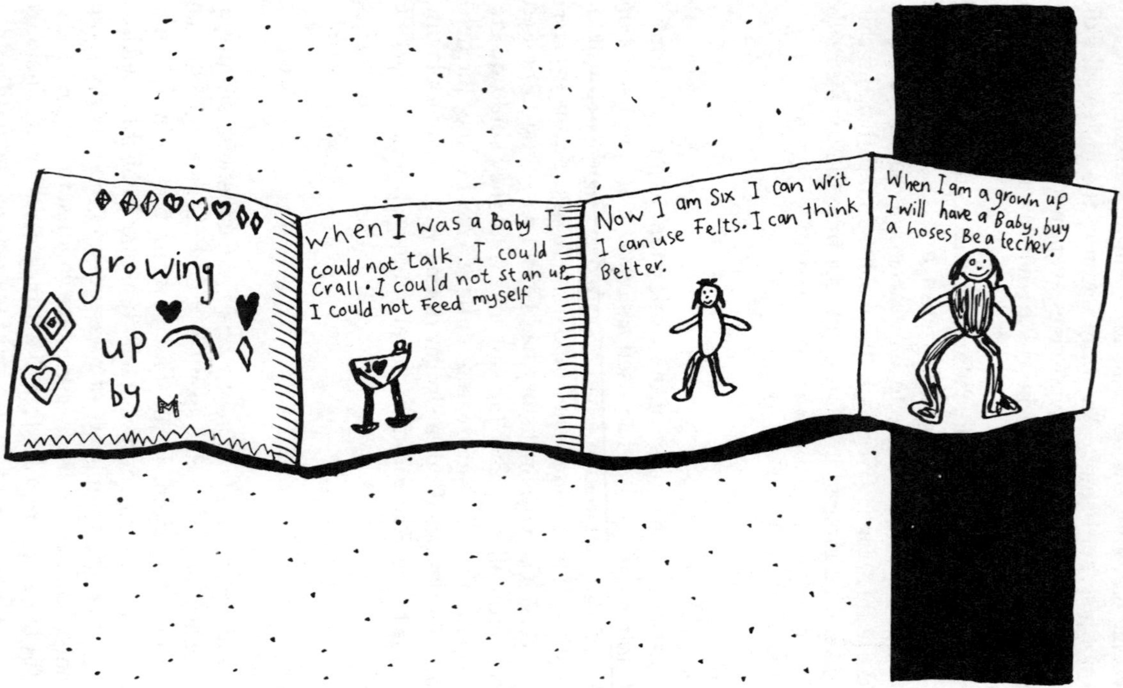

Figure 5.10 Thoughts about growing up

The language-rich classroom

The displays in this classroom, even the small selection shown in the illustrations and described in words show how rich it is in written and visual languages.

In reviewing briefly the words used that were specific to this topic the teacher provided the following: body, skeleton, bones, muscles, veins, blood, organs, heart, brain, lungs, nerves, senses, ear drum, eye socket, breathing, living, internal, joints, size, big (long, tall, heavy). Of these, 'organs' and 'big' presented problems; because 'organs' is a term referring to a group of things all of which look very different, and because the children could not differentiate between long, tall and heavy in descriptions of things as 'big'.

The display for the next topic on light (Figure 5.11) is another example of how rich the study of science is in vocabulary.

Supporting resources

The resources used, apart from the classroom displays, were a video about the human body which covered bones, hair and skin. It supported the children's learning and extended it to areas they would not be dealing with in depth in the topic (animal skin and camouflage).

Book resources included books on the human body which were lent by a parent: the Ladybird books on pets, which have already been mentioned, and a large picture book on the human body.

The equipment needed was relatively simple, mainly stationery items and measuring equipment.

Final note

The children returned to a related topic the following year to learn more about themselves and other living things. The Pine class busy body went with them, and they continued to build their knowledge on to it. Their ID cards also went and these are being used to look at the changes in themselves over a period of time. With continuity from one part of the school to the next often the subject of discussion, it is nice to find such a simple example.

Figure 5.11   Display for starting the next topic – more words

6

The Channel tunnel
YEAR 6 (10 AND 11-YEAR-OLDS)

From overall topic to teaching plans

The school where this topic was taught is in Bexleyheath, a suburb south-east of London close to the rail link running between the Channel tunnel terminus just outside Folkestone to the Eurotunnel terminus at Waterloo in London. At the time, there was debate (and demonstrations) about the route of the rail link, but the route for the tunnel itself had been settled, the construction of the tunnel (or tunnels, as there are three) was well under way and the two sides had already met.

On the UK side, and for most of the stretch under the sea, the engineers were boring through a stratum of chalk marl (a relatively soft but impermeable substance) and, on the French side, through chalk (a soft white limestone, which does absorb water, and can crack). Information available to the public, such as in the small exhibition in Folkestone, focused particularly on engineering problems such as those involved in tunnelling through these types of rocks, in how the tunnel would be lined to stop it collapsing

Planning chart for one term's integrated topic on the Channel tunnel – spring term

English
Research skills
Discussion – present arguments logically
Compile questionnaires
Vocabulary – expand, enrich, develop spelling
strategies
Written language – creative stories, reporting,
letter writing
Reading – stories with tunnels (a challenge!)
Poetry – express ideas and feelings in various
verse forms

Drama
Underground building
Tunnelling, escaping, exploring
Planning rescues

History
The history of the tunnel
Why and when have people wanted to cross the
channel in the past?
How did they do it? Did they succeed?

Maths
Continue to improve and extend basic number
skills
Measurement – length, height, depth of tunnel
Speed of trains
Timetable – length of journeys
Costs – budget, shares, %
Comparison of costs – ferries/tunnel
Collate information from questionnaire (com-
puter database)
Data – proposed use of tunnel, etc.
Improve estimation skills – calculator work

Geography/geology
How we came to be an island
The site of the tunnel – why there?
Types of rocks, suitability, problems
Surveying the sea bed
Map work, tunnel link, choosing a route
Planning implications for the South-East
How man is changing the environment

Music
Music from tubes
How instruments work
Make own instruments

Visits
Folkestone – Eurotunnel exhibition

Speakers
Engineers, surveyors

Science
Metals – investigate different metals, their properties,
characteristics, where found, how made
Test for magnetism – magnetic metals, make simple
compasses
The use of metal in tunnel building (construction,
machinery)
Do compasses work underground?
Environmental aspects of the tunnel
Experiment with different rocks

CDT
Why tunnels are important
Look at different tunnels
How are tunnels made?
What are the problems?
Design a tunnel
Experiment with tunnelling
Design and make a TBM [tunnel boring machine] – will
it work?
Would a bridge have been better? – investigate

Art/craft
Sew a mole (tunnel mascot)
Carve chalk
Accurate drawing
Model making

Figure 6.1 Planning chart for one term's integrated topic on the Channel tunnel

and to prevent water seeping into the interior, as well as on the operation of the tunnel when completed.

The study was planned as an integrated topic incorporating all areas of the curriculum (see planning chart in Figure 6.1) and lasted a whole term. The only subject taught separately was mathematics, with some time each day devoted to it. As can be seen from the chart, however, mathematical skills and understandings were to be used in the topic.

The richness of opportunities for a variety of learning is apparent. There are three historical time-scales; first, the very long geological time-scales of the formation of the rocks in the area and the transition from when Britain was joined to the European land mass to it being a set of offshore islands; second, the time-scale of just over a hundred years from the first serious attempts to make a land route beneath the Channel (the 1881 boring still exists near Folkestone); and third, the time-scale of the building of the actual tunnel. Understanding why and how the tunnel was built as it was requires some appreciation of properties of the rocks, such as hardness, density, absorbency and permeability, alongside an understanding of how information is gained about rocks under the sea and about how routes are surveyed and charted. Consideration of such things as what to do with the spoil from the boring, and what area of land is needed for such a project leads naturally into understanding the impact of the project on the existing environment and to discussion of values. The need to extract, seek out and collate information from books, pamphlets, exhibition labels, videos and people, gives ample opportunity for research skills, for reading, writing, listening and talking.

Anyone used to seeing teachers' planning charts will recognize that this comes from an experienced teacher, who is able in a short space to summarize the main areas of learning and indicate activities which will be undertaken. It contains questions which focus attention on the core of the subject to be studied and which are likely to intrigue the learner. The ones shown on the chart are:

- Why and when have people wanted to cross the channel in the past? How did they do it? Did they succeed?
- The site of the tunnel – why there?
- Do compasses work underground?
- How are tunnels made?

- What are the problems?
- Would a bridge have been better?

These are, in fact, subsets of the 'key questions' selected for the whole topic, i.e.:

- Why is the tunnel being built?
- How and where is it being built?
- Do we really need a tunnel?
- How will a tunnel affect:
  (a) the country?
  (b) us personally?

Key questions are notoriously difficult for beginning teachers to identify. They need to be those questions that get to the heart of the matter and yet are accessible to the particular group of learners that the teacher will be working with. The way in which 'key questions' have to relate two ways – to the subject itself and to the learner – and the ways in which teachers build up their repertoire of questions are discussed further in Chapter 9.

Moving from identifying the learning opportunities in a topic, mapping the concepts, knowledge and skills to be developed and identifying the key questions to be addressed, to planning the order in which things are to be taught is not a simple task and there is no single answer as to how it should be done. Certain things, such as visits, have to be put in the diary early because of the need to book places and transport, and to gain written permission from parents in advance. Timing of a visit within a teaching sequence is crucial. If it is too early in the teaching then the children are not sufficiently briefed to be able to make use of the outside resource, and the time, effort and money involved in organizing the trip are wasted. If it is too late then they go when they have few questions to ask. Many teachers would argue that there is value in two visits: an early one to generate questions and a later one to seek answers, and to ask more sophisticated questions. This is fine if the location is nearby and within walking distance of the school, but not if it requires the booking of coaches and considerable expense (note for instance the teacher in Chapter 3 who took the children several times to the nearby park, but only once to Epping Forest). The precise time for the visit may be determined by external factors such as when there are places available at the site, hence the teacher has to adapt sequences of

Week 1 Jan	Introduction: Looking at maps of the South-East Group brainstorm 'What do I know about the tunnel?'
Week 2 Jan	Pangaea – how we came to be an island *Discover Physical Geography* Hodder and Stoughton
Week 3 Jan	Looking at rocks – different types
Week 4 Jan	Tunnelling – school to swimming pool Civil engineer talk
Week 5 Feb	How do we know what is under the sea? Rock strata and 'how we became an island' work linked Does chalk absorb water?
Week 6 Feb	History of the Channel tunnel – why did it fail? Snow week – collecting 1 m^3 of snow
Week 7	HALF-TERM HOLIDAY
Week 8 Feb	Visit to Eurotunnel exhibition Preparation on European cities; plan journey from Manchester to Paris now and see how to do it with the tunnel
Week 9 Mar	Constructing the tunnel – designing own TBM (programme on moles tunnelling – excellent concept of tunnel building)
Week 10 Mar	Organization of tunnel – the treaty – how it will be run, when it will be open
Week 11 Mar	Operation of tunnel – car and lorry shuttles and other vehicles
Week 12 Mar	Finishing off the folders Completing and testing TBMs 'What do I know about the tunnel now?'
Summer term	One day trip to France by ferry

Figure 6.2 Chronological sequence of the teaching

teaching so that the children are appropriately prepared for the trip. In this topic on the Channel tunnel the teacher planned only one visit to the exhibition centre and put it into week 8, just after the half-term break, of an 11-week topic. (See Figure 6.2 for the chronological sequence of the actual teaching.) The teacher's personal preparation for the visit involved a preliminary visit to the exhibition at Folkestone, when she was able to find out the sort of information in the displays and the people who might be there to answer questions. At this time she designed question sheets for the visit, which matched her objectives and made best use of the exhibition. Such preparation is standard practice at the school; the teachers do not rely on material produced for schools at outside locations without careful consideration as to its suitability for the learning they want to achieve.

The teaching sequence in outline

Before turning to the detail of the teaching, it is worth identifying general features evident in the teaching sequence (Figure 6.2). There is a mixture of learning strategies throughout the topic: practical work alternating with research skills, discussion, writing, watching videos and pencil and paper problem solving. There is the familiar brainstorm at the start which allowed the teacher to find out what the children already knew about the topic. This is followed by a fairly informative two weeks of setting the scene, understanding something of the geological history of the area and the geology as it exists today. In week 4 she posed a problem to the class of planning how to tunnel from the school to the swimming pool which was at the other side of the school grounds. As will be seen later, this produced all the questions tunnelling engineers have to face. This took them, in week 5, to how these questions would look to the Channel tunnel engineers and to consider how people know what is under the sea. At this time also they experimented with one of the rocks (chalk) to help them understand the problems related to the properties of the specific rocks which were encountered by the tunnellers on the French side.

By this point (week 6) the class were beginning to appreciate the complexity of the task and learn some of the reasons why the attempts in 1877–81 and in 1975 failed; hence they were also likely to be prepared for finding from the exhibition how the problems were being solved today. Week 7 was the half-term holiday. The start of week 8, prior to the visit, was devoted to the effect of the tunnel on routes people would take to and from France, and knowing the location of several different European cities (knowledge that was needed to play one of the games at the exhibition).

Much of the data collected at the exhibition became the resource for tackling the last two weeks of the topic, when the management, organization, legal and operational features of the Channel tunnel project were studied in weeks 10 and 11.

The modelling of the TBM (tunnel boring machine) was also wisely left until after the visit, where there had been a good opportunity to look at the machine and understand how it worked.

The Year 6 one-day trip to France was made in the summer term. During this trip children surveyed people's opinions about the use of the tunnel as opposed to the ferry, and also visited the exhibition at Sangatte on the French side, where most of the labels were in French, and viewed the new landscape that had been made out of the chalk spoil from the tunnel.

The teaching sequence in more detail

The topic started with a discussion of a current news item about the Channel tunnel and about protests concerning the route of the proposed rail link. The children split into groups of their own choosing, and talked with each other about what they knew of the Channel tunnel. They then wrote what they knew and the following is typical of the type of account produced: 'The Channel tunnel is a tunnel that goes from England underneath the English Channel to France. I have heard it mentioned on the news lots of times and you can go through it by train. The French side and the English side met in December 1990.'

The general opinion of the class was that nobody knew much and that it would be a good idea to learn about it. The geography of the South-East of England was not known, so considerable work was needed to enable the class to see how close both the terminus, and the straight line from London to the tunnel terminus, were to Bexleyheath. In her weekly notes on her teaching the teacher reported that this lack of knowledge generally within the class was 'a good thing', because 'we can start from the very beginning with the whole class'. Studying maps of the area was therefore one of the first things tackled, along with exercises on how to use compasses to find direction (and how compasses are made). Orienteering exercises in the school grounds proved highly instructive; the first ones were devised by the teacher but when the children understood them, they made up further ones for each other.

There were then two weeks when the class learnt about the formation of continents, earth plates and the Ice Age, and hence began to know that the map of the world has not always been as it is now. The more local effects of the Ice Age, causing Britain to be separated from the body of the mainland by a water channel (although it is still connected to the plate underneath the water), were then studied. The difference between separate plates, and separate pieces of the same plate, is not easy to understand when from the surface they all look like bits of land with water in be-tween. But the difference is important when you are tunnelling; tunnelling between places on the same plate is feasible; tunnel-ling between plates is not!

The fact that there are different types of rock in the earth's crust needs to be appreciated, because the route the tunnel goes may well be determined by the particular rock formations at any point. The study of the formation of rocks in the earth's crust which was undertaken in week 3 set the groundwork for the study of the specific rocks which were in the neighbourhood of possible tun-nel routes. The teacher reported that this topic fascinated the class and she could have done with an expert to help answer all the questions raised, or at least to know where to find all the answers. Between her and the class they put together a considerable collec-tion of rocks, and recognized from preliminary observations and simple scratch tests just how different they were.

The sheer breadth of knowledge that primary teachers have to have is illustrated by this topic. The teacher recorded two of the resources that were particularly useful to her for the first two weeks' work; first was the book *Discover Physical Geography* (Grimwade 1987), and second was a BBC schools programme *Environments* which showed rock formation in coastal areas. This latter is pertinent to the South-East of England as all the rocks are sedimentary and were originally laid down under water.

Week 4 was, in the teacher's mind, one of the turning points in the topic. The task she devised for the children was simply to plan how to construct a tunnel from the school to the swim-ming pool, which was in a sports complex adjoining the school grounds. The journey was not far, but when the weather was rainy or snowy, it was unpleasant. This task turned out to be one of the most fruitful exercises of the topic because it made the chil-dren understand, in a way which was very personal to them, the issues involved in tunnel building. In an initial discussion the class

Things to think about
1 Where is it going?
2 How deep/long/wide does it need to be?
 Where will it start and finish?
4 How will we build it?
5 What will it cost?
6 How long will it take?

What do we need?
A plan
Workers
Digging tools and machines
Building materials

Figure 6.3 Tunnel building – things to think about

Problems encountered
1 Will it fall in?
2 Are there any pipes or cables in the way?
3 How can we be sure we are digging in the right direction?
4 What shall we do with the spoil?
5 Where do we get the money from?
6 Who is going to dig it?
IS IT REALLY WORTH IT?

Figure 6.4 Problems to be faced in tunnel building

listed things they would have to think about in making their plans
and drew up a list of things that they would need (Figure 6.3). The
problems slowly began to emerge; a summary list put together
at the end of the drawing is shown in Figure 6.4. A teacher really
could not ask for much more; the questions are all relevant to
tunnel builders whether going half a mile or 20 miles.

One child's plans are included in Figure 6.5. The accompanying explanation was one of the most detailed, where the child considered the construction and support of the tunnel, the necessary
slope at one end and trapdoor at the other, the number of carriages
needed and the means of moving the carriages through (pulled by
a rope). The rope is to be attached to a winding handle; there is,
however, no information about who will be turning the handle.

The response which I received, when I asked the teacher
how she thought of the idea of the tunnel from the school to the
pool, was typical of what other teachers say about their bright
ideas: 'I don't know, it suddenly came into my head.' There seem
to be preconditions that are often reported: a certain unease that

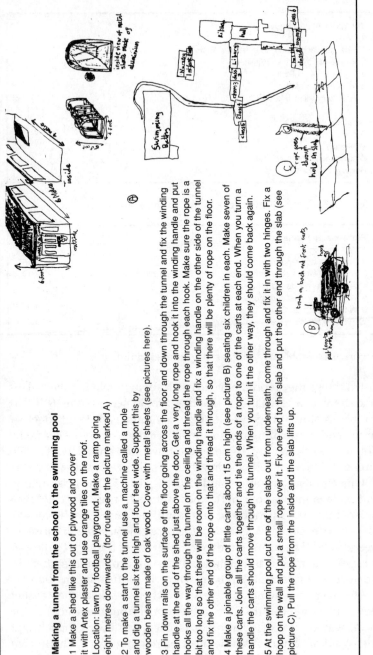

Making a tunnel from the school to the swimming pool

1 Make a shed like this out of plywood and cover it with Artex plaster and use orange tiles on the roof. Location: lawn by football playground. Make a ramp going eight metres downwards, (for route see the picture marked A)

2 To make a start to the tunnel use a machine called a mole and dig a tunnel six feet high ard four feet wide. Support this by wooden beams made of oak wood. Cover with metal sheets (see pictures here).

3 Pin down rails on the surface of the floor going across the floor and down through the tunnel and fix the winding handle at the end of the shed just above the door. Get a very long rope and hook it into the winding handle and put hooks all the way through the tunnel on the ceiling and thread the rope through each hook. Make sure the rope is a bit too long so that there will be room on the winding handle and fix a winding handle on the other side of the tunnel and fix the other end of the rope onto that and thread it through, so that there will be plenty of rope on the floor.

4 Make a joinable group of little carts about 15 cm high (see picture B) seating six children in each. Make seven of these carts. Join all the carts together and tie the ends of a rope to one of the carts at each end. When you turn a handle the carts should move through the tunnel. When you turn it the other way, they should come back again.

5 At the swimming pool cut one of the slabs out from underneath, come through and fix it in with two hinges. Fix a hoop on the wall and put a small 'rope over it. Fix one end to the slab and put the other end through the slab (see picture C). Pull the rope from the inside and the slab lifts up.

Figure 6.5 One child's plans for the tunnel from the school to the pool

something different is needed for all sorts of reasons (in this case because the topic was becoming too teacher-directed) and a willingness to try something new. Also, when dealing with things on a very different scale from pupils' normal experience, a 'bridging task' is needed which relates both to their existing experience and the new knowledge they are to learn; this local tunnel served the function of such a task.

About this time parents of children about to join the school were making preliminary visits, and amongst them was a civil engineer who was more than willing to come and talk to the class about tunnel building. She chaired a lively discussion about the advantages and disadvantages of bridges and tunnels and showed the class how to navigate in a straight line underground (where compasses won't work).

She was also able to provide geological maps of the area on both sides of the Channel, which proved useful when the children were looking at what types of rock would need to be dug out at the different sites. Week 5 was devoted to the specific geology of the area and particularly to the question of how people know what is under the sea. This was set as a problem to the class in rather the same way as the school tunnel problem. The children came up with a range of ideas – divers, submarines and shafts – some very futuristic. At this point the teacher made them think back to the work they had done on how Britain became an island separated from the mainland to think about the likely strata under the sea. She had as a resource not only the geology maps referred to above but posters from various exhibitions, some specifically written with children in mind. These show quite clearly the strata continuing under the sea with the same rocks mirrored either side.

By now the children knew that the chalk was considered more of a problem than the chalk marl for several reasons: it cracks easily, it absorbs water and it is harder than chalk marl. They devised scientific tests to appreciate the extent of the problems. The investigations were relatively simple but were all devised and carried out by the children themselves. These included:

- finding the difference in the weight of chalk when it is wet from when it is dry;
- finding out how much water chalk will hold;
- measuring how much water is absorbed by chalk by pouring water on to chalk in a jar and marking the initial water level.

The water level was then checked again several hours after the chalk had absorbed the water;
- finding out how rapidly powdered chalk settled in a mixture of chalk and water.

These were all relevant because the means of getting the chalk out was to grind it up, mix it with water and pump it out into tanks where the slurry had to settle.

The historical study in week 6 provided the opportunity for the children to appreciate that projects of this sort require carefully worked out cooperation between the two countries (the 1877–81 tunnelling ceased because the French and English could not agree about a completely different matter, i.e. who should govern Egypt). They also require a lot of money (the 1975 boring had to stop because at the time of the world oil crisis the British government could not afford to carry on).

Week 6 was the week when snow happened to fall and the teacher had the inspiration to take advantage of it, by asking the class to collect it into a pile to try and make one cubic metre. In fact the children never quite managed to collect enough, which helped them to register just how much material there is in one cubic metre and to begin to have some idea of the sheer volume of spoil that was being dug out of the tunnel every day (1100 cubic metres) and which had to be dealt with in one way or another.

Week 8 was the week of the visit to the exhibition. By this point the children were armed with considerable information about, and understanding of, the problems of tunnelling and hence were likely to be able to make use of the technical explanations which featured in the exhibition. They had done less on the effect of the tunnel on travel times and routes, so at the start of the week the teacher set an exercise of finding details of the current journey from Manchester to Paris. This particular journey was selected so that the children could compare it with the journey when the tunnel was open, which featured in one of the displays at the exhibition.

The journey from the school to Folkestone takes less than an hour, so it was possible to spend three hours at the exhibition and still fit the whole excursion into the normal hours of a school day. The question sheets devised by the teacher covered the technical side (materials and construction of the tunnel linings, size of the tunnel); differences in transport arrangements for cars, lorries, caravans, coaches and bikes; the total system of tunnels and termini; the advantage of the tunnel for train passengers; the frequency of trains to both Paris and Brussels; operational control such as dealing with passports and buying tickets; measures proposed to stop the spread of diseases such as rabies; the effect of the tunnel on tourism in the region; the history of the tunnel and military concerns about having a tunnel between England and France; several exercises requiring collection and manipulation of data about proposed number of cars, passengers, etc. and about journey times and distances. Finally they had to go to the top of the viewing tower from where they could see the site where the terminus was being built and work out where everything would go.

On return to school, thank you letters had to be written both to the parents who had accompanied the school party and to the Eurotunnel exhibition staff:

Dear Mrs Clark
I am writing to you to say thank you very much for helping looking after us when we visited the Eurotunnel exhibition. I was pleased I went because it helped me learn about the tunnel and it will help me with my work. I liked the train set best because it showed you where the tunnel went and how it worked.
Yours sincerely
M

Dear Eurotunnel
Thank you for letting us visit the exhibition. I learnt a lot of things to do with the tunnel especially the times of how to go from Britain to France by the Eurotunnel. I also enjoyed the game that was in the centre. I was a couple of minutes out. I especially enjoyed the Marcus Mole quizzes above the gift shop. Also I enjoyed the painted world where you had to search for Marcus, in the world. I also enjoyed the film.
From
K

Week 9 was devoted to the theme of actually constructing the tunnel, using the information gleaned to date. The teacher commented that 'the work done previously on chalk proved very useful as the children had a good understanding of the problems of the French.'

It included watching a nature programme on moles which gave an excellent concept of tunnel building. The week included the start of two practical tasks: making models of TBMs and sewing toy moles (Marcus the Mole was a tunnel mascot, and appeared as the 'explainer' on posters about the tunnel, especially those pre- pared for children). The TBMs at the exhibition had generated a lot of interest; it is not until you stand next to these machines that you can appreciate just how large they are and how powerful they must be. The class were keen to have a go at making work- ing models. The models the children made incorporated a base on wheels so that the machine could move down the tunnel as it was bored, and various solutions to the boring tool (screwdrivers were one solution). The boring tools were powered by electrically driven motors and they were tested on a sandy bank in the school grounds. Inevitably the children hit a lot of problems in making these but learnt a lot in the process. One thing they had not thought about until they tested their models was that you need some means of reversing the tool to pull it, and the spoil, out.

The final two weeks were spent completing the practical tasks; the children used the information collected at the tunnel and in the poster display at school to discuss further the organizational and operational features of the tunnel project, to prepare a class poster of the tunnel and to complete their project folders.

Figure 6.6 shows some questionnaires that the children wrote. They did in fact play an important part in the project. The chil- dren had decided to survey people's opinions about the tunnel. They had thought that it would not take long to write the ques- tions, only to find that it was a very difficult task to write questions which effectively elicited the information they wanted. The teacher had a lot of discussion with the class first about what it was they wanted to know and then about what question would be suitable. The questionnaire was given to people in the area, people travel- ling on the ferry to France and to relatives of the children who lived in other parts of the country. The difference in answers from people who did not live in the South-East was noticeable; they automatically thought the Channel tunnel was a good idea and would be happy to travel in it.

This difference in perspective when things are on your doorstep was noticeable in another way. The teacher found that the children were very anxious about the threat of rabies spreading, via foxes and other animals being able to walk through the tunnel. This fear was heightened by the presence of foxes in the school grounds.

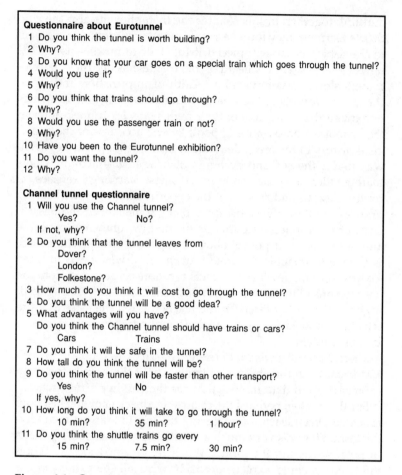

Questionnaire about Eurotunnel
1 Do you think the tunnel is worth building?
2 Why?
3 Do you know that your car goes on a special train which goes through the tunnel?
4 Would you use it?
5 Why?
6 Do you think that trains should go through?
7 Why?
8 Would you use the passenger train or not?
9 Why?
10 Have you been to the Eurotunnel exhibition?
11 Do you want the tunnel?
12 Why?

Channel tunnel questionnaire
1 Will you use the Channel tunnel?
     Yes?   No?
  If not, why?
2 Do you think that the tunnel leaves from
     Dover?
     London?
     Folkestone?
3 How much do you think it will cost to go through the tunnel?
4 Do you think the tunnel will be a good idea?
5 What advantages will you have?
  Do you think the Channel tunnel should have trains or cars?
     Cars   Trains
7 Do you think it will be safe in the tunnel?
8 How tall do you think the tunnel will be?
9 Do you think the tunnel will be faster than other transport?
     Yes   No
  If yes, why?
10 How long do you think it will take to go through the tunnel?
     10 min?   35 min?   1 hour?
11 Do you think the shuttle trains go every
     15 min?   7.5 min?   30 min?

Figure 6.6 Questionnaires written by children

The intensity of questioning and seeking out of information about the preventive measures was impressive. Eventually the children were satisfied with the proposed precautions and even explained these carefully to others who shared their original anxiety.

Summary

My narrative in this chapter has followed a chronological sequence. I am, however, still aware of the jigsaw metaphor I used in Chapter 3 to describe my finding out about other people's teaching: fitting the bits together piece by piece until they all make sense and link together. In this chapter the metaphor fits also the children's learning: they found a whole range of information relevant to the topic and slowly pieced it together to make sense of the news items periodically heard on radio or television. The children's folders slowly accumulated a wealth of information and ideas: the factual reports of the Channel tunnel construction; drawings to explain the construction; their own plans for tunnelling from the school to the swimming pool; letters; accounts of the geological history of the area; ideas about how one might survey what was under the sea and accounts of how it was actually done; mathematical exercises on journey times; mapping exercises on routes; designs and reports of the experimental work with chalk; drawings to show the landscaping plans at the French and English ends of the tunnel; descriptions of the environmental concerns and solutions; and poems about being in a tunnel. The reader will have to imagine the wealth of material which was in these folders from the few brief extracts reproduced here and from the descriptions of the activities in which the children were engaged. Right at the end of the term the teacher asked the class to write what they now knew about the topic and these accounts were also in their folders.

There was also a wealth of poster resources accumulated which had become, in the absence of books about the tunnel, the main source of up-to-date information for the children's research.

For the teacher, perhaps the clearest feedback showing just how much had been learnt came during the trip to France the following term. This was very much a family trip with as many parents as possible joining the group. When they visited the exhibition the children could explain precisely what all the exhibits were about, without having to read the labels (many of which were in French). They were pleased with how much they knew and how much they could explain to their parents (who were, of course, impressed). They also visited the area of Sangatte, which was originally a flat area, but which had been reshaped with the chalk which had been dug out of the tunnel in water, and then used to form hills. It made an interesting contrast to earlier studies they had made about routes through Kent when they had learnt how routes had had to follow the geography of an area. Now people no longer needed to 'follow a landscape' because they could alter it quite dramatically. Again the children were able to explain the whole process to their parents.

Children's accounts of what they had learnt

The accounts of what the children had learnt, written at the end of term, were at least three times the length of those written at the start in January, and some were much longer. They contained a lot of detail, as in the following two accounts:

> When the French started to build their tunnel they found out that they would have to go through chalk and that chalk absorbs water so at their end of the tunnel they put rubber linings so that the water would not go into the tunnel . . . the soil they got out at the English end they poured down a cliff and made a nature reserve with it. At the French end they had chalk so they mixed it with water and then made hills.

> The workmen use tunnel boring machines to build the tunnel and they follow a laser beam to make sure they're going in the right direction . . . England and France used to be joined under the sea, so now we will be joined again . . . To start off with the people have to dig a shaft . . . The French have special TBMs because they have to go through chalk and chalk can crack and the water would come through.

Finally reproduced below is the full account from one child who wrote not only about the things that had been learnt but about his awareness of how much he had learnt:

The Channel tunnel
You should have seen me on the first day of term only knowing a few things about the tunnel, but things have changed!! I know all about Pangaea the supercontinent which was the world millions of years ago and I know about the Ice Age, when the world sank and when the Channel was formed and England was four-fifths covered with ice! I understand about the environment and I think planting oak and ash woodland is a good idea and the land will be landscaped. They are also offering double glazing to people who live nearby to reduce noise. I know all about the treaty and I'll mention a little about it. Well, the treaty was signed by Margaret Thatcher and President Mitterand on the 29/7/87. The tunnel will be operated by Eurotunnel for 55 years. I know about igneous rocks and sedimentary rocks. Igneous rocks are formed when hot molten rock cools down, sedimentary rocks are usually

found in the oceans and are formed by bits of rock, and dead
plants or animals, I know such a lot that I'm going to need
another page!! I know about the history of the tunnel as well.
Albert Mathieu had an idea about a tunnel. His idea was a
horse-drawn transport throughout the tunnel. His idea also
included a tall chimney that raised above the sea so fresh
air could come in. Another person interested in tunnels was
Thome de Gamond. He said that he would have to make
geological surveys before you could build a tunnel and it
will take ages to write it so look through my topic folder for
more information. So, happy reading!

7

The river Thames

YEAR 4 (8 AND 9-YEAR-OLDS)

Introduction

The topic of the river Thames described in this chapter, like the previous one on the Channel tunnel, came from the Aquatech Project, in which attempts were made to explore the potential of links between industry and schools in a modest way. The industries concerned had some connection with water technology, and hence schools participating took a theme related to water as the basis of these studies. In order to collect information, teachers were asked to keep a log file of the teaching, in which they recorded plans, successes, frustrations, resources used, and things learnt. In addition a selection of the classroom products were displayed in an exhibition also showing the outcome of the project. Both the files and the exhibition panels afforded valuable information about teaching; they became the initial source of data for the preparation of Chapters 6 and 7 of this book. They were of course supplemented by discussions with the teachers and by the teachers commenting on the first drafts.

The nature of the Aquatech Project was such that participating schools attempted to set their teaching in the context of a specific real-life project. The teacher in this chapter's case study chose the topic of the river Thames, as it forms an important geographical feature in the neighbourhood of the school (the Abbey Wood Estate in the London Borough of Greenwich), and many children knew little about it other than its name. Within this specific topic, however, the teacher selected two main themes that had applicability to water in general. These themes were the movement *of* water, particularly in channels, and movement *in* water. The first concerned questions of flow, water currents and the way material is carried in water; the second included the study of means of propulsion of both fish and boats through water. Because the topic investigated a specific river, the class studied the river's geography (where it started, where it ended, its meandering shape, the changing depth at different places and locations of sandbanks and shallow areas) through maps.

The class of 8 and 9-year-olds was a multi-ethnic group, with several children for whom English was a second language. There were 26 children in the class, 14 girls and 12 boys. This was the second year that they had been taught by this teacher; she had already instilled in them considerable independence of action and thought, and they were used to the way that she organized the teaching and learning. She reports that had this not been the case (and had she not had several years experience) she would not have tried having a river of water in the classroom, made by an electric water pump circulating water from a bucket to the start of a plastic gutter pipe – as well as another water trough where floating and sinking experiments were under way, a paddling pool for testing boats, and a role play area in the form of a large yacht in the corner of the room. She also recognized that taking in fish from the fishmonger for close observational drawing, coping with the inevitable fishy smell about the place, and the need to keep the fish overnight in the refrigerator so that the work could be completed over two days, did require considerable goodwill on the part of her colleagues.

Planning ideas and resources

The overall map of the topic, produced during a planning weekend when several teachers met to consider possibilities, is given in Figure 7.1. This plan has strong elements of science, technology and language, with some history and geography; the subsequent work did integrate these elements with considerable success. There was no intention of making the topic cover all areas of the curriculum; mathematics was done separately, for instance. Art and drama became more integrated in the work than is apparent. The main ideas to be developed were clearly identified at this stage.

The advantage of such a plan is that it is possible to see straight away the resources that need to be collected: navigation and Ordnance Survey maps of the area; books about rivers, including those which refer to changing landscapes, the management of rivers in general and the history of the river Thames in particular; books about boats which focus on key features of design in relation to function; books about creatures which live in rivers with information about how their structure helps them to live in, and move through, water; stories about travel in boats (real and imaginary); fish and other water creatures (does the teacher get alive or dead creatures, or in this case, both?); possible places to visit (a fishing trip and Greenwich Maritime Museum were listed as possibilities); a water trough for trying sinking and floating; equipment for making the class river, including materials for making dams; technology tools for making boats; consumable materials for the models; a paddling pool for testing boats; a mop and bucket, and plenty of newspaper to put on the floor to absorb water spills.

More detailed plans

Figure 7.2 shows her next planning chart. The layout and detail of the original has been retained, but it has been typeset rather than left in her handwriting, because of the need to reduce it for publication. It is worth pausing here to identify features revealed in this second plan.

Observational drawing and writing has been selected as the starting activity, with the teacher being quite clear about the ideas she would be developing. She planned a discussion of differences *and similarities* (a point she emphasized in discussion with me) between humans, fish and shellfish. Within that section, the fi' of the key questions appears: 'What defines a fish?'

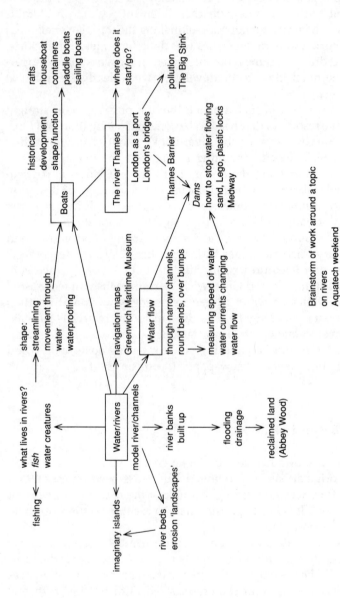

Figure 7.1 Plan from initial brainstorm

Topic   ***The river Thames – water/rivers***

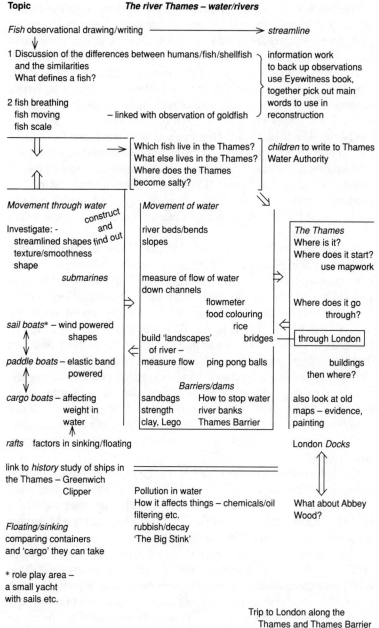

Fish observational drawing/writing ⟶ *streamline*

1 Discussion of the differences between humans/fish/shellfish
and the similarities
What defines a fish?

2 fish breathing
fish moving   – linked with observation of goldfish
fish scale

information work
to back up observations
use Eyewitness book,
together pick out main
words to use in
reconstruction

Which fish live in the Thames?
What else lives in the Thames?
Where does the Thames
become salty?

children to write to Thames
Water Authority

Movement through water
construct
Investigate: -   and
streamlined shapes find out
texture/smoothness
shape
          submarines

Movement of water

river beds/bends
slopes

measure of flow of water
down channels
                    flowmeter
                    food colouring
                    rice

The Thames
Where is it?
Where does it start?
          use mapwork

Where does it go
          through?

*sail boats** – wind powered
          shapes
paddle boats – elastic band
          powered
cargo boats – affecting
          weight in
          water
rafts   factors in sinking/floating

build 'landscapes'   bridges
of river –
measure flow   ping pong balls

Barriers/dams
sandbags   How to stop water
strength   river banks
clay, Lego   Thames Barrier

through London

          buildings
          then where?

also look at old
maps – evidence,
painting

London *Docks*

link to *history* study of ships in
the Thames – Greenwich
          Clipper

Floating/sinking
comparing containers
and 'cargo' they can take

* role play area –
a small yacht
with sails etc.

Pollution in water
How it affects things – chemicals/oil
filtering etc.
rubbish/decay
'The Big Stink'

What about Abbey
Wood?

Trip to London along the
Thames and Thames Barrier

Figure 7.2   A more detailed plan of the topic

The teacher gave me three reasons for starting with the observational drawing. The first is that it starts from an object, rather than something more abstract. The second is that all the class can be working together and have a common experience, which can then be used as a basis of discussion with the whole class. (She knows that later, as the topic develops, children's activities diverge.) The third is that close observational drawing provides information *about* the object directly *from* the object with the teacher giving little input. However, to take the learning further, and to enable children to move from specific experiences to generalizations or unobservables, the teacher used a range of useful questions: 'Mine has spots' 'Do they all have spots?' 'Mine has clusters of round things' 'Could they be eggs?' (A useful follow-up text to this conversation was Charles Reasoner's book *Who's Hatching?*, 1995).

The teacher was clear at the planning stage about ideas that she would bring out in the discussions of the drawings: 'breathing', 'moving' and 'scales' were all marked on the plan. She was also clear that she would make sure that some questions would link observation to explanation, such as those about what the parts of the fish enable it to do. This would lead to the study of books and study of an actual fish (a goldfish) to find answers (both of which activities are incorporated in the plan). The plan also shows several activities which require the children to use the information they are learning in a new way so that they show that they understand it (see for instance on the top right-hand corner of the plan, 'information work to back up observations', 'together [as a class] pick out the main words', 'to use in reconstructing writing').

The links through to the later part of the topic were indicated by the arrows. Questions about what fish live in the Thames, what else lives in the Thames and where the Thames becomes salty lead through to the study of the Thames. Note again a language exercise which is built in, namely the writing of a letter to the Thames Water Authority for information. The concepts of streamlining, driving mechanisms (moveable tails) and balance mechanisms (fins) are linked to the work on the movement of boats through water, the two-way arrows indicating the expectation that the later work will inform the earlier work and vice versa. The means of learning has been written across the corner, i.e. 'construct and find out'.

Timetable of activities in the topic

Week	Fish /prawn	Sink/ float	River (1)	River (2)	Paddle boats	Role play	Map work	Sail boats
4	■							
5	■							
6		■						
7		■						
8	HALF-TERM HOLIDAY							
9			■		■	■	■	
10			■	■	■	■	■	
11			■	■	■	■	■	■
12			■	■	■	■	■	■
	EASTER HOLIDAY							
End of April/ early May						■		■

Figure 7.3 Time sequence of topic

I will leave the reader to track through the rest of the chart to find further key questions, linking threads, and ideas for experiences, along with new features which were not hinted at in the first planning sheet (Figure 7.1) but which appear in the second one.

Figure 7.3 gives the time sequence of the teaching, indicating the main blocks of time when the different sections of the topic were tackled. The starting date for each indicates the point at which a new resource and set of activities were put into the classroom and introduced to the class as a whole. Week 9 required a major reorganization of the classroom to accommodate the tank and the river, and half-term provided a useful point for the transition. Thinking carefully about the spatial organization of the class at different points is crucial.

Having the time sequence drawn out in this way showed one other important feature I might otherwise have missed, namely the increase in the diversity of science activities occurring as the topic progressed (obviously there were other non-science activities going on). To start with there was only one science activity, then this increased to two; after half-term there were four and finally six, reducing after the Easter break to two as the topic came to a natural end and new studies were started.

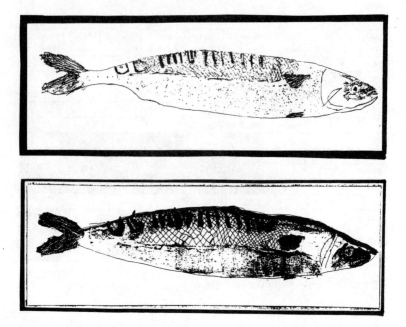

Figure 7.4   Children's drawing and painting of a mackerel

Classroom products

The remaining illustrations in this chapter feature some of the products which were displayed at the Aquatech exhibition. Like the products in 'Rabbit's House' (Chapter 4), they provoked me to enquire into the role the teacher played in helping children to produce them. The summary notes which the teacher kept in the Aquatech file at the end of each block of work, and my subsequent conversations with her, provided the answers. The narrative of the chapter therefore follows from my questioning.

Drawing, painting and writing about the fish

Figure 7.4 shows one child's drawing and another child's painting of a mackerel, while Figure 7.5 shows a third child's writing about the structure of a mackerel and a fourth child's writing about the links between structure and function. Unfortunately the paintings are not in colour, but the originals show the detailed

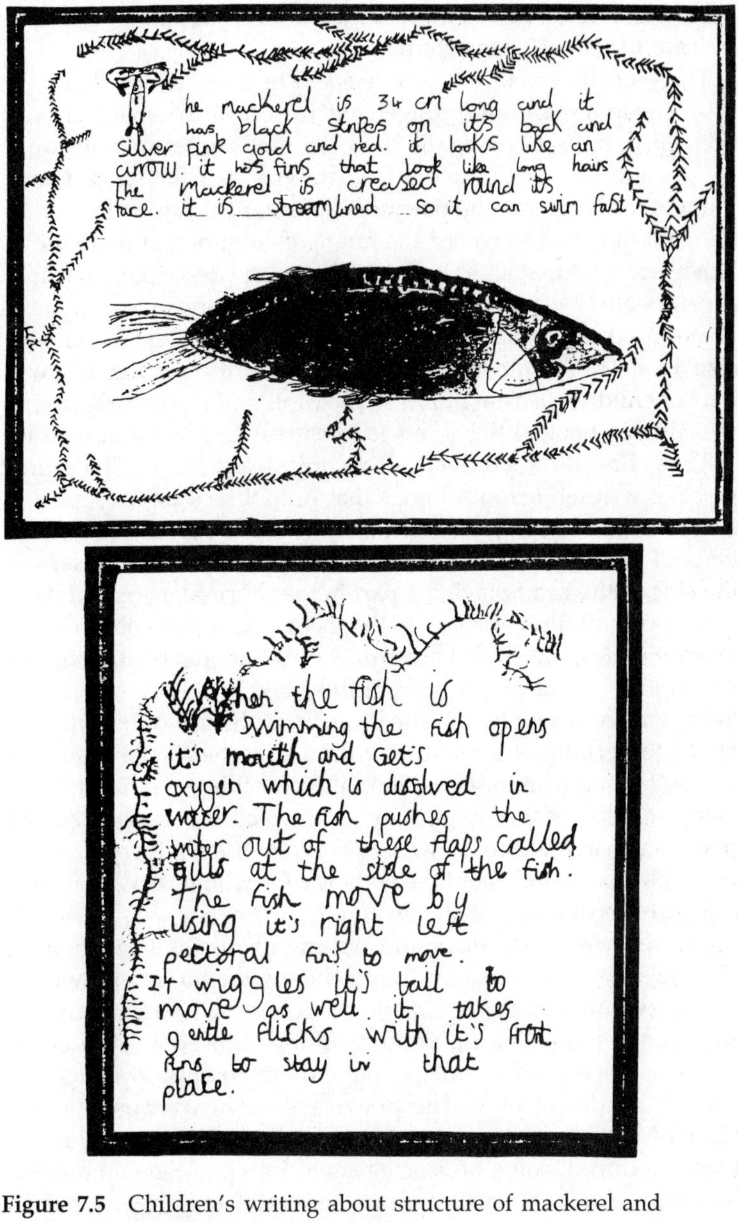

The mackerel is 34 cm long and it has black stripes on it's back and silver pink gold and red. it looks like an arrow. it has fins that look like long hairs The mackerel is creased round its face. it is ___streamlined___ so it can swim fast

When the fish is swimming the fish opens it's mouth and Gets oxygen which is dissolved in water. The fish pushes the water out of these flaps called gills at the side of the fish. The fish move by using it's right left pectoral fins to move. It wiggles it's tail to move as well. it takes gentle flicks with it's front fins to stay in that place.

Figure 7.5 Children's writing about structure of mackerel and movement of fish in a classroom tank

observation of colours of the fish accurately and skilfully recorded by careful use of watercolour.

Three of the pieces of work need to be seen as different children's responses to encouragement to record in whatever way they liked. In the drawing the child recorded successfully features, shapes and textures. (The original drawing was life sized, which made it easier to get one part in proportion to another.) Painting allowed the child to record the range of colours that there are in a fish which at first sight looks just grey. The descriptive writing, accompanied by a painting, brings in the use of precise language to point out important features and of measurement to indicate size. Note the illuminated letter T that starts the writing; this was part of children learning to raise the profile of their work, saying effectively: 'Look at this – this is interesting – come and read it!'

These first three products all record observations. The fourth piece of writing includes things that cannot be seen (oxygen dissolved in the water, and the fact that the fish is able to get the oxygen out of the water, with the opening of the mouth and flaps at the side of the head playing a part in the process); names of parts (gills, pectoral fins); along with things that have been observed by watching the goldfish and confirmed by looking in books (tail and pectoral fins used to move, front fins used to stay in one place). What we are seeing here is the product of the use of information books to back up observations, with the teacher picking out key words, talking with the class about their meaning and the children using these new words in their writing (cf. Figure 7.2 detailed planning chart). Before the writing was undertaken there was considerable discussion about the audience for whom they were writing and the purpose of the writing.

The drawings, paintings and writing about the dead prawns (Figure 7.6) show similar features, there were no live prawns to watch swimming. These drawings were much larger than life size. Again the colouring in the painting showed a lot of attention had been paid to mixing the correct colours to match the various shades of pink. The prawn paintings were used as the basis of batik work; lengths of dark cloth with pink prawns on were produced, some of it being sewn into padded embroidery. The move from observation drawing to stylized artwork has an important purpose because children have to focus on the important detail which has to be retained in the transformation.

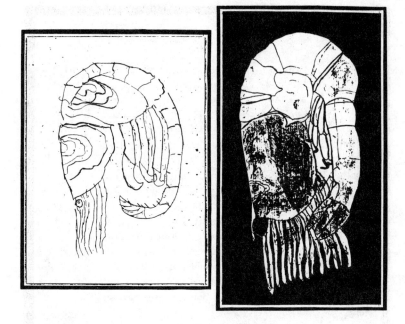

Figure 7.6 Children's drawing and painting of a prawn

After the children's first 'response to the fish', the teacher wrote: 'There are some fantastic drawings and paintings that can be developed into batik. Written descriptions are less interesting than conversation ... I need to develop observations through to information and explain some specific vocabulary.' In the first week she had encouraged the children to think about why things were as they were (i.e. the function of scales, of the tail, of the gills, of the mouth opening), but they had fuller discussions, followed by searches for information and observation of the goldfish in the second week, and their writing began to be richer in detail and vocabulary. The examples of writing that are included in both Figures 7.5 and 7.7 came from the second week of the teaching.

In the discussions with the class, the teacher wanted to help reinforce the idea that fish were just another living thing like human beings, but at the same time had their own particular characteristics. She therefore talked about both similarities and differences between humans and fish. In her questioning about

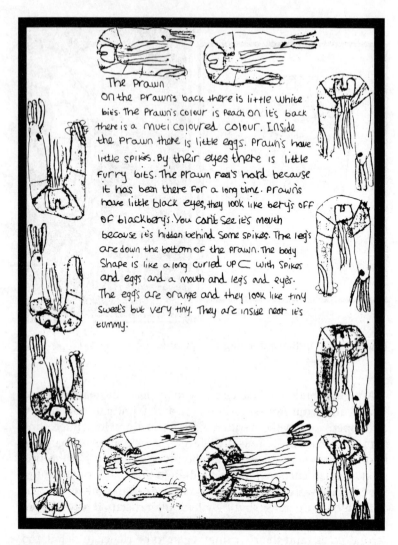

The Prawn

On the Prawn's back there is little white bits. The Prawn's colour is peach on it's back there is a muti coloured colour. Inside the Prawn there is little eggs. Prawn's have little spikes. By their eyes there is little furry bits. The Prawn Feel's hard because it has been there for a long time. Prawn's have little black eyes, they look like bery's off of blackbery's. You can't see it's mouth because it's hidden behind some spikes. The leg's are down the bottom of the prawn. The body shape is like a long curled up ⊏ with spikes and eggs and a mouth and legs and eyes. The eggs are orange and they look like tiny sweet's but very tiny. They are inside near it's tummy.

Figure 7.7 Children's writing about the structure of a prawn

the similarities between humans and fish, the children found it very difficult to find anything similar, because they saw themselves as so very different from fish. When she pointed out that both humans and fish had two eyes and that both of them moved, the children thought that she was tricking them in some way, thinking 'She can't really be serious, we're nothing like a fish!'

Some things which seem obvious can take a long time and a lot of experience for children to change in their thinking. It is also important to help children think about *relevant* similarities (neither fish nor humans live on Mars but that is not very relevant).

When the teacher was talking about the fish 'breathing' by taking in water, this presented even more of a puzzle than the similarities discussion, because the process is so different from breathing in humans, especially because if humans take in water the one thing they cannot do is breathe.

The questions 'What defines a fish?' or 'If something is a fish, what do you expect it to have, or do?' were at first challenging, but slowly the children analysed and put into words the characteristics of a fish. Their initial difficulties illustrate the problem that everyone has of explaining a self-evident fact (children by the age of 8 believe they know whether something is a fish or not, without having to explain it, unless of course if someone asks them if a shark is a fish!).

The improvement in the writing came not only from further discussions, but by the teacher using a simple technique of children reading their writing out to other children. 'There was huge value in the class reading back their writing to the whole class'; she explained that they seemed to hear their own mistakes, recognize that they had left things out and then go and improve it by themselves. The activity did not always involve the whole class; it could be done by small groups 'conferencing'.

Use of information books was not as simple as it sounds, because she found that most of them were 'completely inappropriate for the age group'; they were either patronizing and simplistic or too technical. The Eye-Witness series had excellent photographs but difficult text that required mediation by the teacher. She used this to model how to cope with such a text, by identifying the difficult words and discussing their meaning, or looking them up in a dictionary.

A letter was written to the Thames Water Authority at about this point in the topic to find out about fish in the Thames. What needed to go into the letter was discussed with the whole class, but only two children put letters together and only one was sent (for the obvious reason that the Authority would hardly appreciate having letters from every child in the class!).

It is often later that a teacher gets evidence of what has been learnt and assimilated. This teacher became aware that the children

had understood about the action of the tail of the fish in pro-
pelling it forward and the significance of the streamlined shape
from an incident which occurred two or three months later in the
summer term. 'When the class were studying tadpoles, they quickly
focused their attention, without prompting, on how the tadpole
swam, how it moved its tail and on its streamlined shape. Other
features were not so quickly noticed.' It is also a useful reminder
of the importance of previous experience in aiding observation.

Floating and sinking

On the planning sheet (Figure 7.2) floating and sinking appear
in the bottom left-hand corner. This work was set up at the start
of the second week, while the work on fish was still under way.
Equipment comprised a table with a water trough and a range of
practical activities related to boat shapes.

The activities included making objects (such as corks and containers) float at different levels in the water to become aware that
there is not a sharp cut-off point between sinking and floating;
making boats out of pieces of aluminium foil, of the same size
and shape, to find shapes that will float without overbalancing
one way or another; loading these boats until they sank in order
to find the shapes that carried the most; testing other containers
to find out the shapes which would carry the most before sinking. Some very different shape aluminium boats were made with
surprisingly (to the children at least) different capacities, which
forced discussion about what variables were particularly significant for having a high carrying capacity.

This was one of the activities that the teacher would have liked
to follow up more systematically. The children were testing with
non-standard units and hence it was difficult to compare one boat
with another with any reliability. She considered, nevertheless,
that the children did have a better understanding of sinking and
floating than previously; they appreciated that the statement 'heavy
things sink and light things float' was not sufficient. They knew
there were other factors which came into play, particularly the
shape of the vessel. They knew that it was possible to alter the
level at which things floated and that by extending the shape in
some way it is possible to increase the carrying capacity. She
judged that only about four or five children would have any idea
of density, even at the intuitive level.

Map studies

The map studies started after half-term with children trying to use maps to answer the following questions:

> Use the different maps and atlases to find the river Thames.
> Follow its course and see where it goes.
> Can you see where it started?
> Can you see where it ends?
> Where does it go? What places does it pass?
> What bridges and tunnels can you see? (Look around London)

As the ability to read maps and take information from them increased, then the maps became more sophisticated. They were a major prop in the role play area as they were consulted on the various 'journeys' taken in the classroom yacht. Navigation maps showing the sandbanks in the Thames estuary were particularly popular, and children came to realize the importance of understanding the detail on these if you are trying to navigate a safe passage up or down the Thames from or into open sea.

Classroom river (model 1)

Figure 7.8 shows the 'river' in the classroom. The work started with another set of questions which helped focus the children's initial observations and trials. As time went on, however, children tried many more activities. The starting questions were:

> What happens to the 'river' if the slope is steep or very gentle?
> What happens if the 'river' is wider? or narrower? or bendier?
> What does the water do if there is something in the way?
> What happens if it is completely blocked?
> How fast is the 'river' going? Where is it fastest?
> Can you split the 'river' into two or three?

The initial exploration of water flow then focused on flow down different slopes, in different guttering and round obstacles. The children worked in threes and were left to investigate together with only occasional intervention from the teacher (she used questions such as 'what about . . . ?' and 'what do you think would happen if . . . ?'). The findings were drawn together in class discussion with group feedback in order to suggest further investigations.

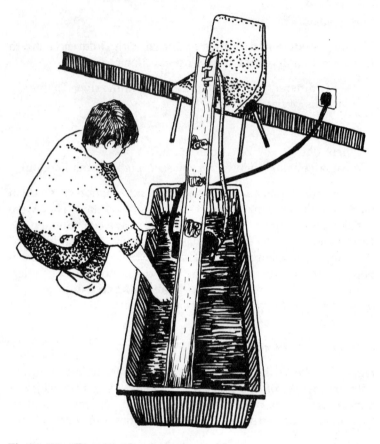

Figure 7.8   'River' in the classroom

In their observations the children were fascinated by altering water flow, observing cross-currents, constructing waterfalls and jumps, and they found things around the classroom to act as obstacles.

In order to explore how fast the water travelled they used small floating objects and stop clocks to test and investigate. There was some frustration here, because the river was not on a large enough scale to produce results of any kind. (Floating objects had got to the bottom before the children were able to time them.) Discussion of the difficulties, however, led to suggestions of alternative worthwhile investigations that could be done; this took the children into what is marked on Figure 7.3 as 'River model 2'.

Classroom river (model 2)

The children had suggested making the river look more like a river by giving it bumps on the river bed and bends on the side. These were constructed out of Plasticine and clay. The clay proved much more effective than the Plasticine, which tended to slip and was more resistant to work into the shape needed. There was fruitful discussion and observations of water flow over bumps and round bends. The children observed the wearing away of the clay and slowing down of the water at various places. They used food colouring in the water to help them see the water and the flow rather better. Their detailed observations were then written up to accompany drawings. Having done their own writing, the children then discussed as a group important things to select to summarize their findings. Like other language exercises enabling children to review their learning, the teacher reported this to be immensely valuable to them.

Paddle boats

The making of the paddle boats was a highly disciplined activity. The paddle boats were made eventually from corroflute (rigid enough to withstand the forces of the wound-up rubber band, sufficiently non-resistant for young children to be able to cut it safely, waterproof so that it can be put in water, of sufficiently low density that it will float), although other materials were offered – one child did try cardboard first.

To get this activity started, the teacher showed the children the mechanism of the paddle and a simple shape. She discussed with them what they could do differently. They came up with the possibility of having the paddle in a different place, using different material and altering the shape of the boat.

The making of the boats occurred over a period of four weeks. The making, as could be seen by the children's drawings and written accounts, involved several stages: the drawing of the plans (based on a design given by the teacher) on squared paper; transference of the plan to the corroflute, by means of pricking a pin through the paper; cutting of corroflute with a Stanley knife to make the main body of the boat, and then cutting out the paddle; attachment of the paddle by means of a rubber band. Finally the boats were tested and accounts written of the whole process. It

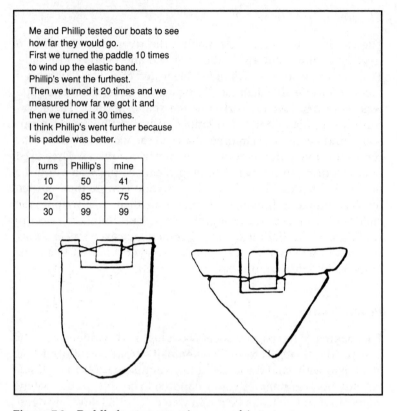

Me and Phillip tested our boats to see how far they would go.
First we turned the paddle 10 times to wind up the elastic band.
Phillip's went the furthest.
Then we turned it 20 times and we measured how far we got it and then we turned it 30 times.
I think Phillip's went further because his paddle was better.

turns	Phillip's	mine
10	50	41
20	85	75
30	99	99

Figure 7.9 Paddle boats comparisons – a fair test

is interesting to note the different foci of the writing: how boats were made; what had to be done to make them work (winding up the rubber band); which way the boats went; how the paddle made the boat go; and in one case, how a problem was solved. The writing not only focused on the making, however; the highly structured input on how to make the boat meant that the focus could be science rather than just technology. A successful boat was essential if the children were going to devote some of their thoughts to how it worked. For a fuller account of four children's drawing and writing about this task, see Frost *et al.* (1993).

Figure 7.9 shows one of the investigations where two children compared the performance of their boats and began to consider what variables might account for the differences. In this case, and in others in this chapter, it is evident that considerable

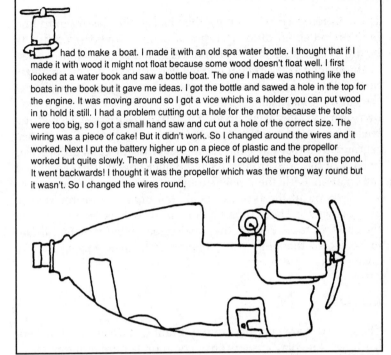

had to make a boat. I made it with an old spa water bottle. I thought that if I made it with wood it might not float because some wood doesn't float well. I first looked at a water book and saw a bottle boat. The one I made was nothing like the boats in the book but it gave me ideas. I got the bottle and sawed a hole in the top for the engine. It was moving around so I got a vice which is a holder you can put wood in to hold it still. I had a problem cutting out a hole for the motor because the tools were too big, so I got a small hand saw and cut out a hole of the correct size. The wiring was a piece of cake! But it didn't work. So I changed around the wires and it worked. Next I put the battery higher up on a piece of plastic and the propellor worked but quite slowly. Then I asked Miss Klass if I could test the boat on the pond. It went backwards! I thought it was the propellor which was the wrong way round but it wasn't. So I changed the wires round.

Figure 7.10   Electrically driven boat from a Year 6 class

learning in science often emerges from 'construct and make' activities because of the direct involvement of the child with the material world.

The account of a boat made by a child in the Year 6 class in the same school (Figure 7.10) has been included for comparison with the work of the younger children. The writing shows the ability of the older child to share not only the doing with the reader, but the thinking as well. It is also clear that the older children had a far wider choice of materials and designs at their disposal, a choice that the Year 4 children could not have coped with. The constraints put on the task for the Year 4 children by the teacher seem eminently appropriate, and yet she left those small areas of choice, which are so important for children to take over some of the thinking.

Information work on boats

The children used what books they had in the classroom to find information about different types of boats, why boats needed to be different shapes and also to develop the beginning of a sense of chronology as far as boat making was concerned. The organization of this activity was important. Whereas for most activities the children had chosen who to work with (or worked on their own), for this they were divided into five groups and each group was given a different boat to research. The groups were then regrouped so that one child from each of the original groups was in each of the new groups. Each member now had to share their information with their new group members, so that everyone learnt about all the types of boats (an organization referred to as 'jigsawing'). These presentations provided the motivation for the children to make sure they understood what they had found in books, so that they could explain it to their colleagues and answer their questions.

Role play

The role play area became an important feature of the children's learning. Role play corners are a common feature of infant class-rooms but less common in the junior classes. It was established initially in several drama sessions where children role played being in a small yacht in different conditions. They had to sail away from the mainland and act out some of the adventures that they had at sea in which they had deep water, rough water, islands, shipwrecks and pirate attacks to cope with. They also wrote post-cards to people from the ship to give accounts of their voyages and adventures. Thereafter children were allowed to use the role play area during the day as they wished, to develop their own stories. The teacher found that the children became completely involved; and as they learnt more and more about boats, rivers, and water flow, so she found their new knowledge and vocabulary was built into their play. Somehow the role play experience allowed them to browse through their new vocabulary. The boat slowly acquired life jackets, a fishing rod for catching food, maps (especially the navigation maps), and snorkel and flippers for fishing just below the surface. It had a mast, with sails which could be hoisted, and a rudder.

The collection of ongoing weather records, largely thought of as part of their mathematics work, contributed to the data and vocabulary that they could use in the boat.

Sail boats

The sail boats were a second 'construct and find out' activity, similar to the paddle boats, with the teacher hoping that children would be able to compare the performance of boats with different sails. The design was drawn initially on squared paper and, as before, was transferred to the actual construction. In terms of construction and design, a lot of new skills were taught or old ones consolidated, using different materials and tools (saws, drills, knives, etc.). The children were increasingly aware of the importance of careful measurement, and were more independent in their organization.

There were some frustrations in the organization of the testing of the boats. The battery-powered fans were completely unreliable. In the end a hairdryer was used to create a wind, but children found it difficult to compare results and get any satisfactory data. In any case the teacher found the children keener to construct a boat than to plan for differences and comparison.

The teacher as role model – reviewing learning

The teacher believes very strongly in the value of reviewing learning and modelling discussion to aid learning. She therefore made the children take stock at least twice a week with the whole class. She used questions like 'What have we learnt?' 'Did everyone find that?' 'Did it always happen?' 'Why did that happen?' 'Why do you think that is like that?' (what she calls 'hunting the "because" '). She encouraged children to do the same, for example in the shared writing from the work on the classroom river.

Organization of the activities

To some extent features of the organization have already emerged in the account. Groupings for most activities were fairly fluid, with children choosing with whom they worked. The teacher kept control of what the children did by each day indicating on a diagram on the board what activity each child would start on, where they would go next and then the point at which they could have some choice over what they did. The diagram was in the form of a double wheel. The inner wheel had on it the core activities; the children had to move round it and complete everything before they moved to the outer wheel. The outer wheel had extra activities and promoted considerable independence. Children's names were put against different activities to indicate where they should start for the day, and they knew that this determined a large part of their daily activities.

Most of the decisions about who should be doing what were determined by the ongoing assessments she was making and the need to ensure that children tackled all areas of learning; some decisions were also determined by the resource constraints, for instance she could only have a small group working at the river at any one time, or making and testing boats.

Despite this organization to allow children to work at their own pace, and hence often to work on their own, she nevertheless brought the whole class together on several occasions during the week for the review of learning, for tackling new work, for administration and for story reading.

Teacher's overall evaluation

I have built the teacher's evaluations of each section into the early part of the chapter, but reproduce here her reflections on the whole topic in which she raises issues which have been identified by other teachers in the other chapters.

It was a successful topic but raised several questions/issues for me:

1 Often what the children learn/benefit most from is not reflected in the volume of written work, or detail. Much of the value of working with the river model was the physical tactile experience of experimentation with water in a new way. Children spent hours trying different things and learnt a lot but what they learnt is summed up in a few sentences of shared writing.

2 Children tend not to write about what they tried that 'didn't work', and so really only focus on the 'successful' thing they did, however much encouragement they receive from the model set by the teacher.

3 It is easy to underestimate the amount of time children need to experiment/investigate in their own way. I was conscious of time limits and so some activities were not followed up as far as they might have been.

In light of her second point it was interesting to note that she did in fact meet with some success in encouraging at least one child to write about things that went wrong, in the task of making and testing the paddle boat: 'It never worked. I put some sticky-back plastic on it to make it waterproof but it went all soggy. So I decided to make one out of plastic. I did the same as last time, and it went brilliantly'.

8

Seeing and light
YEAR 1 (5 AND 6-YEAR-OLDS)

Introduction

In preparing this chapter, I worked initially from the teacher's own written account of her teaching, supplemented by her subsequent comments on my first draft. At the time she was writing she was particularly interested in the ideas that children bring to their learning, the way they try to make sense of new experiences and the way they develop new ideas. She recorded in considerable detail some of the classroom conversations and events, following closely at one point the progress of four pairs of children. I have quoted extensively from her writing, so any quotations not otherwise acknowledged are hers. The chapter ends with what was the final section of her original account, in which she reflects on the process of trying to develop ideas in other people's minds. It is fitting that as this is the last in the series of case studies, it should end with the direct voice of a teacher.

The topic was taught in the second half of the autumn term. The children had already been in school for one, two or three terms in the reception class in the previous school year. English was not the first language for over 50 per cent of the class and the teacher could not speak any of their home languages. Development of language, and particularly of vocabulary, was therefore an important part of her day-to-day work, seeking to improve children's confidence to express their ideas both orally and in writing in what for many of them was their second language. She made a point of listening carefully to make sure that as best she could she was hearing the ideas some of the children were trying to express behind their limited knowledge of English.

The presence of a language support teacher for a high proportion of the week also allowed the teacher to work with small groups in considerable depth, initiating (and recording) the conversations and interventions which were essential to support the children's thinking. In her teaching generally she tried to maintain the appropriate balance between the need to direct and steer children's thinking while providing children with opportunities to test and sort out their own ideas. With this class, with so many children still only 5 years old, she had a clear picture of the need for structure:

> Though the children had experienced science activities previously, this particular topic was organized in a more structured, developmental way, in terms of skills, processes and concepts. I felt they needed clear teacher guidance and a firm structure within which to work, to provide security when tackling new concepts and skills, and because the class as a whole was not 'awash' with initiative.

The topic of Sight was prescribed in the school topic plans. It was part of a whole-school topic on Light and Darkness in which different classes focused on different aspects. The teacher had some autonomy over how she tackled the topic and what she attempted to achieve. She planned initially to cover five main areas in the following order:

- the physical features of the eye;
- the purpose of eyes;
- the link between seeing and light, i.e. that we cannot see without light and that the pupil of the eye is a 'window' through which light enters;

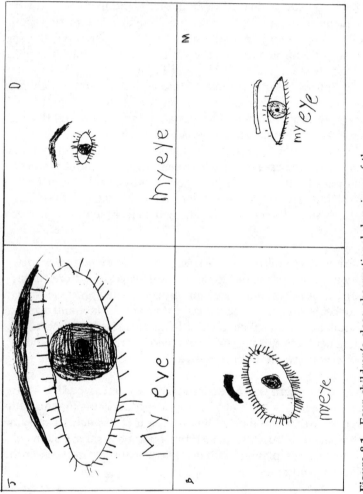

Figure 8.1 Four children's close observational drawings of the eye

- materials that you can and cannot see through (transparent, translucent and opaque);
- individual differences in sight (including eye tests).

In the event the last two areas had to be abandoned, because of the extended experience that was necessary for the earlier work on the 'purpose of eyes'. The order, particularly of the first three, was significant: working from something concrete which the children could see and draw, to the more abstract idea of purpose, and then to an attempt to understand that there is a link between two separate things, i.e. between seeing and light. She was aware of the research on children's understanding of the connection between seeing and light from the SPACE project on light (Osborne *et al.* 1990) (see Chapter 2) and that she was likely to have limited success in this area.

Learning about the physical features of the eye

Close observational drawings; data collection and analysis

Apart from an initial discussion in which the children told the teacher what they knew about seeing (they had two eyes, they were unsure about the colour of their eyes, and they used them for seeing), the first activity was close observational drawings of their own eyes, using a mirror to see themselves (Figure 8.1 shows four of the drawings). The drawings show the careful observation that young children can make. Most of the drawings show eyelashes on both top and bottom lids, the pupil in the centre of the iris, the colour of the iris, the iris extending to the two lids, redness at either end of the eye, an eyebrow above the eye and a reasonable shape for the eye itself. These drawings were also copied with remarkable care on to the covers of their I-Spy books (books in which they drew objects that they could see beginning with different letters of the alphabet).

The original drawings were in colour and were displayed on charts so that the differences in numbers of children with different coloured eyes were immediately apparent. The colours of the eyes of all the children in the class were also recorded by another means, by the children writing their names in the appropriate columns in the chart shown in Figure 8.2. The preponderance of

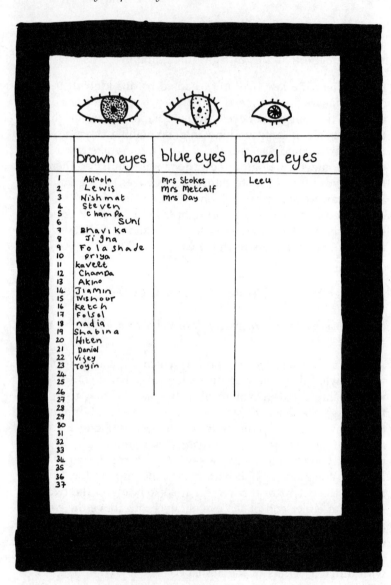

Figure 8.2   Chart to record distribution of colours of eyes

brown eyes was easily noticed, and the children came up with a hypothesis that eye colour might be linked to ethnicity. They subsequently collected data from the other two Year 1 classes, and identified that on the whole their hypothesis was reasonable.

Model of the parts of the eye – naming the parts

A small group in the class, working with a support teacher, made the low-relief eye shown in Figure 8.3, and this was used for discussion about the names of the various parts of the eye and what those parts did. The discussion extended to the position of the eyes in relation to the rest of the body.

Conversations and interventions

The very first conversation revealed how little the children had noticed about their eyes before the teaching started, so the later realization that so many of the class had brown eyes was to them a real discovery and a source of considerable surprise and amazement. The teacher urged them to talk about why they were surprised. It emerged that the children had assumed that anyone who had fair hair had blue eyes and that all White people also had blue eyes, theories which were easily challenged by the evidence in front of them. In response to the question 'Why do you think there are so many children with brown eyes?' one Asian boy suggested 'because we are Indian'. When the children looked round the class (about 80 per cent of whom were of Asian origin) they spotted that 'Indian children always have brown eyes', again a point which they had not noticed before.

The teacher asked the children to consider how they could test their idea, and in doing so we note one of the cases of an intervention where the teacher is pressing the group to take their thinking one stage further. They suggested the idea of surveying the whole school to see if it was true for a larger group – a suggestion the teacher took up, but reduced the scale of the survey to the other two Year 1 classes. A recording chart was drawn up by the teacher, because it was beyond the scope of the children to cross-reference two variables. With some help from the teacher the children were able both to collect the data (she took two children at a time into the other classes) and to put this data on to the chart. The form of recording required the children to use a tally for the counting, marking one stroke for each child in a particular

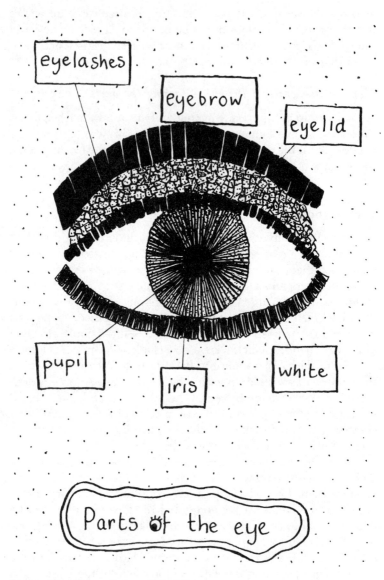

eyelashes

eyebrow

eyelid

pupil

iris

white

Parts of the eye

Figure 8.3   Low-relief model of the eye

category and then counting up all the strokes at the end. Interpretation was considered by the whole class through discussion with the teacher. The boy who made the original hypothesis was delighted to find that his hypothesis was borne out by the additional data.

The teacher's role during the original drawing exercise required her merely to watch and identify any problems and quietly intervene: 'If a child had any difficulties I intervened by drawing their attention back to the real thing, encouraging them to correct their own mistakes.' The commonest difficulty in this particular exercise is that children tend to draw their mental image of an eye, without checking it against the real thing; hence the iris is often drawn as a small circle with lots of white round it, when in fact it is rare that you can see white above and below the iris. The teacher had to do little prompting to start children comparing their eyes. 'Though working individually the children soon became aware of similarities and differences through chatting with friends and comparing pictures.'

The model eye provided several language exercises. One involved learning the names of the parts of the eye and talking a little about what the parts did; a second involved spotting language links in many of the words, e.g. 'eyelid', 'eyebrow' and 'eyelash' all contain the word 'eye'. A third was a conversation about one set of eyelashes which happened to have been stuck on the wrong way round; the teacher asked the children to account for why this was wrong. One child's response was 'because you would blink, and blink and blink', indicating quite clearly that he understood that this would cause a lot of irritation to the eye. The teacher wrote in reflecting on this episode:

Comments such as this, and those contributed by the children throughout the topic, increased my awareness of the wealth of ideas children have and their ability to reason with unexpected logic. This in turn motivated me to take much more account of their ideas as valid and relevant. The children furnished further examples when my support teacher discussed the position of eyes in relation to other parts of the body: 'What would happen if our eyes were at the back of our heads?' One child, K, replied: 'We couldn't look where we were going' and another, A, said 'Our feet face the other way, so we would bump into things and fall over.'

Summary of the first phase

At the end of the first phase of the topic, the children had a far better knowledge of the eye than they had at the start. They had learnt this to a large extent from their own observations. They had put together data from the whole class and identified patterns in the data (the high proportion of brown eyes). With teacher support they had come up with a hypothesis to explain the patterns in the data and collected further data to test the hypothesis. They had also learnt the vocabulary to describe parts of the eye and discussed the working parts and the position of the eye. They had used three different forms of a table: the posters on which the pictures of the eye had been collected; the lists of children with blue, brown and hazel eyes; and a more sophisticated table on which they had recorded nationality and eye colour.

Learning about the purpose of eyes

Reading and discussion

The start of the second phase involved reading many topic books about the eye and discussing as a whole class 'what our eyes help us do'; but a short written exercise in which the teacher asked the children to write 'We use our eyes to . . .' produced disappointing results. 'Their writing and pictures were uninspiring, being mostly preoccupied with the simple act of looking or seeing, rather than extending beyond that, i.e. to read, see colours, to write, paint, etc.' She made the decision that the children needed far more experience of actually trying activities with their eyes open and closed than the one investigation she had originally planned. The children's reactions to the subsequent activities and the conversations that she had with them about the results bore out the wisdom of this decision.

Testing to find out what children could and could not do with their eyes open and closed to learn about the purpose of eyes

There was now, therefore, quite an extended period when the children were involved in carrying out investigations. These fell into two categories: those that the teacher designed and which were tried out by all the children in the class, and those planned by a small group of children who were particularly keen to extend their investigations further. Those planned by the teacher required the children to find out if, with their eyes closed, they could:

- cut out a circle properly;
- draw faces better than with their eyes open;
- follow a straight line of masking tape on the hall floor;
- tell shape and colour.

The investigations planned by the children, working in pairs, were designed to find out if, without looking, people could:

- write better than with their eyes open (L and M);
- put together a jigsaw (B and L);
- see pictures in a book (S and N);
- build a bird table better than with their eyes open (D and M);
- put together a picture of a rabbit out of sticky paper (C and A).

Conversations and interventions – investigations planned by the teacher

Figure 8.4 shows the results of one of the first investigations tried, that of cutting out a circle with eyes shut and eyes open. Note first, the simple means of recording: it is an early form of a table with two columns each headed by a symbol of an eye indicating whether the circle was cut with the eyes open or closed. The use of sticky paper for the circles meant that the result of the investigation could be transferred immediately to the recording sheet. The recording sheets could also be displayed on the wall so that children could see a pattern in the results, i.e. that everyone was having difficulty in cutting out a circle.

This particular investigation, being the first, turned out to be instrumental in changing children's ideas and giving them pause for thought. They had started by making the predictions, with considerable confidence, that they would be able to cut just as good a circle with eyes shut as open, that they would be able to draw faces and tell colour with comparative ease. The teacher reported:

> After watching one or two of their friends their confidence in their predictions began to dissipate. Their responses varied:

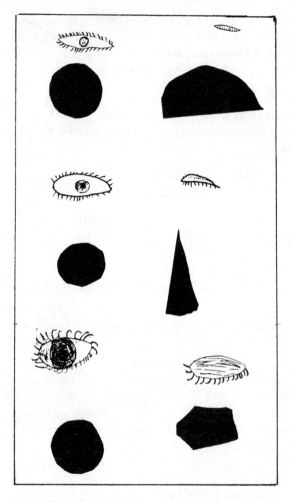

Figure 8.4 Results of 'Can we cut out a circle as well with our eyes shut as with them open?'

K, after viewing his attempt at cutting while blindfolded said with amused despair 'It's very difficult' . . . Not only did they test their own predictions, but the visible recorded results forced them to question what were firmly held convictions.

The teacher wrote that they began to wonder that 'if they couldn't cut out well without looking, would they be able to do other things?'. Predictions about subsequent investigations were

more tentative, 'consisting of many more "nos" and rather hesit-
ant "not sures" ', showing that the children were applying what
they had learnt to another situation. The results of drawing faces
showed similar difficulties to cutting out a circle.

In talking to me about this topic the teacher could still recall
vividly the looks of puzzlement and amazement on the children's
faces as the results began to emerge. These investigations were
some of the 'significant events' in this teaching sequence; those
points at which a teacher recognizes that a new level of curiosity
has been aroused; that existing experience and thought is being
challenged.

There was also anxiety – in some cases, quite serious. It is
important to realize that such events can make children feel very
unsettled. There are two situations combined in these investigations which make children sense that they are not succeeding and
are 'wrong'. The first is making predictions only to find that their
predictions are wrong, and the second is failing to cut out and
draw properly. They both contributed to the children's unease,
but a recognition that they were all in the same boat with their
predictions helped to ease their feelings; and the fact that the
teacher joined in all the investigations, showing that she could
not do things with her eyes shut either, was also important. As
the topic went on, these anxieties faded.

Many of the conversations, especially in the early investigations,
focused on 'cheating' and 'fairness' of the way investigations
were carried out. 'Cheating' could involve letting the blindfold
slip slightly so that the experimenter could in fact see; it was
always the other children who could recognize whether others
were cheating by the extent of their success in completing an
activity. The children began to decide their own criteria for deter-
mining fairness, for instance, they insisted on tying blindfolds
tight on everyone. Alternatively cheating could be that different
clues were given in games such as 'Blind Man's Buff', a game that
was played as part of PE. The teacher reported: 'A was quickly
denounced because he kept talking which according to C was
unfair: "You can tell who he is because of his voice".' These
discussions were, however, productive; by the time the children
came to try to walk along a straight line marked on the hall floor
with masking tape, there was no need to use blindfolds, the
children just shut their eyes. They enjoyed the feeling of trust
that had developed between them, and the teacher was aware of

the children's growing recognition that cooperation and fair play were essential if the activity was going to be of any value.

The last of the investigations devised by the teacher involved trying to decide whether shape and colour can be identified just by feeling. Coloured plastic shapes were used and one was put secretly into a 'feely' bag. The children had to put their hand in and decide which shape and what colour the object was. One child insisted that he could feel that a particular object was blue, because, he explained, it was slippery like another blue one they had tried earlier.

Conversations and interventions – children's own investigations

The change to investigations devised by the children afforded the teacher insight into their understanding of the planning process, which of course cannot be seen from investigations devised by the teacher. The first of these investigations occurred quite spontaneously. After trying the investigation on drawing faces, L and M rushed off to see if they could do any better writing instead of drawing. They started by writing the alphabet, only to come unstuck because they could not write all of it with their eyes open, let alone closed. When the teacher suggested that they write something that they knew, M suggested writing 'I am . . .' followed by their name. They went away and completed the test with ease. Because of the policy of not including individual children's names in the book, the results cannot be included, but they met with more success than in drawing the faces with their eyes shut; the writing was not as good, however, as with their eyes open.

The children who planned their own investigations were effectively self-selected. They had shown great interest in the work and taken considerable initiative. They were not, in conventional terms, the brightest or most intelligent – there were others who were more skilled at reading and writing – but they were incredibly enthusiastic about the experimental work. L and M were of course in this group. The teacher put them in pairs (B and L, S and N, D and M, A and C) and asked them to devise more tests that they could try out on themselves and other people.

B and L decided to find out if people could do a jigsaw with their eyes closed. They started with a plastic number jigsaw, in which numbers had to be slotted into appropriate slots on a board.

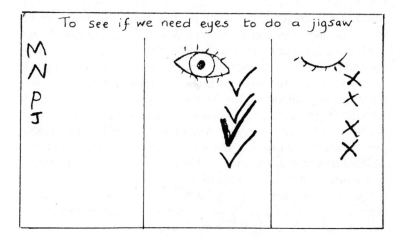

Figure 8.5 Results of picture jigsaw used by B and L to find out if people could do a jigsaw with their eyes closed

This proved relatively easy – B and L realized this was so because it was easy to feel the shapes. They then moved to a picture jigsaw, and the teacher helped them to draw up an appropriate recording chart (see Figure 8.5); they were of course able to make suggestions about what chart they needed themselves because it was similar to the ones used for earlier investigations. When they looked at the results, they could say that people could not do jigsaws with their eyes closed, and this the teacher wrote for them on the bottom of the chart. In talking with the other children about the design of the investigation they recognized that the jigsaw that they had chosen had rather too many pieces, so the test took quite a long time. If they did it again they would try to find one with fewer pieces. This provides a nice example of very young children being able to evaluate the design of their own investigations.

S and N wanted to know whether people could identify pictures in a book with their eyes closed. 'They failed to find a "satisfactory" picture in a book so disappeared next door to draw their own, in "secret isolation".' They drew two pictures, and the subject was asked what was on each one. The teacher raised the question of whether the person tested would do it with their eyes open or closed first. After considerable thought they realized that if it was done with eyes open first, people might remember what was on the pictures, so they had better do it with eyes closed first.

A and C's investigation involved children trying to make the face of a rabbit from sticky shapes. A and C cut out the shapes in advance and put them in separate pots (eyes, face, ears). They also cut out sheets of paper on which to stick the shapes to make the face. The reader needs to imagine the laughter and amusement that accompanied these trials as eyes and ears were stuck all over the place, and in one case half the face missed the page altogether. One child did, however, manage to make a reasonable picture which led to discussion of how this was so. The children realized that he was able to focus his mind on the feel of the pieces and work from tactile information.

The reader also needs to imagine the conversations that occurred between the children and teacher in refining the design of this investigation. The design, as completed, is quite sophisticated. It is relatively quick to do, the results can be seen easily and the record kept and displayed.

The investigation into building a bird table devised by D and M proved more problematic than the others because of a complication which they inadvertently built into it at one point. They had headed off at first to make a 'world' out of 3D shapes (this was a new concept which had come out of discussion). 'They finally – with much prodding – decided to see if people could build a bird table from 3D shapes, while blindfolded.' D decided this was too difficult without instructions, so proceeded to draw some. When the first subject was asked to try the investigation, D wanted to know if he could build a bird table with and without the instructions, while M wanted to know whether he could do it with and without a blindfold. The poor subject ended up rather confused, with D and M not understanding why! They had drifted into the trap of trying to test two variables at the same time, and it took a lot of help from the teacher for them to be able to simplify the experiment. D and M's confidence and enthusiasm revived as she helped them out. She also provided the format for recording the results although she did use their suggestions.

In reflecting on these episodes of children trying to devise their own investigations, the teacher wrote:

> This was relatively unfamiliar territory for the children, which
> involved me contributing a tremendous amount of support
> guidance and motivation, while refraining from telling them

exactly what to do. It was exhausting work, con
ing, making tentative suggestions, yet with
them space to work things out for themselve
been impossible without support to preoccupy th
ing children.

Summary of learning about the purpose of eyes

The teacher's own summary focuses on the intensity of involvement of the children:

> The critical reflection, investigation and process skills which
> were involved in these activities speak for themselves. The
> communication between the partners and other children was
> a delight to hear and rewarding in itself. Added to which the
> children came away with an immense amount of satisfaction.

Learning about the link between seeing and light

Before the teacher moved to exploring a link between seeing and
light, she decided it was important first to have some activities
to help the children think about light itself. She asked them to
draw sources of light at night and during the day so that she
could find out what ideas they had, a technique also used by the
SPACE project.

Exploring the effect of light (and no light) on seeing and on the eye

The two main practical activities used here were devised by the
teacher. The first was to find out if the children could see if there
was no light at all. The second was to discover the effect of light
on the size of the pupil of the eye.

Finding a place where there is no light is not easy. The teacher
simulated what often happens when people go on guided trips
into caves. At one point a guide gets everyone settled comfortably
deep underground, where no light drifts in via shafts, and then
says, 'For about three seconds you are now going to see what abso-
lute darkness looks like', and proceeds to turn off the underground
electric lights. Pitch black is indeed an unusual experience for

ost people, and it is slightly eerie. The members of the party on the tour usually have complete trust that the guide will turn the light back on after the allotted time, and the trust is warranted. The teacher's nearest approximation to a cave was the large stationery cupboard in her room. It had no windows, and when the door was shut and the light turned out it was reasonably dark (she had nowhere where it was completely dark). In it the children were surrounded by brightly coloured paper and card and packets with writing on. Like the guides in the caves, she settled the group with the light on and told them she would only turn the light out for a short time, which she did. She knew that the first exercise would cause excitement and 'spooky' feelings. The first visit was done therefore as a language exercise, asking the children to talk (and later write) about what it feels like to be in complete darkness. Only after the excitement had worn off did she repeat it with a focus on science. 'What can you see now?' (with the light on). The children told her all the things they could see first. 'Keep your eyes open, so they are still working. When I turn the light off I want you to look around and tell me what you can see.' When it became evident that however wide they opened their eyes, they were having difficulty seeing things, the children began to appreciate that perhaps the light did have something to do with seeing.

Amongst the various discussions that were provoked by this experience was the subject of sources of light. The teacher asked the children to draw things that they thought gave off light. The discussions with individuals about what they had drawn are described below. (Eyes – either their own, with drawings similar to ones drawn earlier in the term, or cat's eyes – feature in many of the drawings.)

The teacher also designed an experiment on the pupil of the eye. She wanted the children to know that the black pupil in the centre of the iris was a 'window' into the eye, that light went into it, and that it changed size from small when there was a lot of light, to large when there was little light. The experiment involved the children looking at the sizes of the teacher's pupils and their own pupils when they were in dark and light places. She had made the pictorial scale for measuring size on which the children wrote L and D for the sizes of the pupils in light and dark places respectively (Figure 8.6). The children simply held the gauge next to their noses, just below the eye, and found the size of dot which

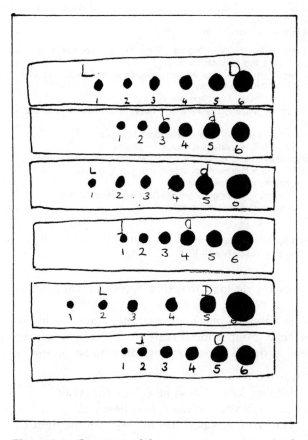

Figure 8.6 Gauges used for measuring eye size (with results marked)

matched the pupil size the best. As the organization of such an activity is often the key to its success, especially with such young children, I have included the teacher's exact sequence of teaching for this part of the work in Figure 8.7. It is noticeable that she has started with a demonstration of what to do, has worked with the children and then left them to try it by themselves.

Conversations and interventions

The teacher had kept detailed notes of responses from the children, and although transcripts of conversations are notoriously

---

How does light get into our eyes?
Relating pupil size to available light

(i)   Return trip to dark cupboard – reminding the children that we need light to see
(ii)   Ask: How do you think light gets into our eyes?
(iii)   Cloakroom: I cover my eyes, count to ten, remove my hand, children observe any
       change in pupil size. Repeat with children.
(iv)   Using torch: observe effect of bright light on pupil size
(v)   Investigate using pupil gauge (gauge held up to nose): – dark cloakroom versus
       bright light torch
(vi)   Comparison of results – general trend for everyone? Discussion
(vii)   Return to classroom: refer to non-fiction book on pupil size
(viii)   In pairs or singly children then explore the classroom/cloakroom using a mirror –
       trying to find places where their pupils are bigger or smaller. They come and tell me
       and relate it to 'darker' and 'lighter' situations.
(xi)   Discussion of too bright light being dangerous i.e. never look at the sun.
       What do we use to protect/shade our eyes?

Figure 8.7 Teaching sequence for work on relating the size of the pupil of the eye to the available light

difficult to interpret, I decided that they would be valuable to include here.

In sharing their observations about what they could see in the cupboard, this small group noticed both the difficulty of seeing and the fact that in dim light everything looks monochrome.

M: It was too dark to see.
D and L: Everything looks the same colour (lights off) . . .
              because you can see the colour less.
A: . . . The writing is best [i.e. to see] with the light.

Amongst the responses to 'How do you think light gets into your eyes?', there is the idea that light comes to the eyes. One child shares information from another source (sister) about what the pupils really are (holes), while another makes the suggestion that perhaps they are not holes at all, but only look like holes because they are black:

K: Light comes to our eyes.
N: Light shines in our eyes.
N: My sister says pupils are holes.
A: . . . They look like plastic . . . they look like holes because
     they are black.

In another group, they talk of the light getting into the eyes because they are open:

H: It shines.
B: When we see light it gets in our eyes.
P: . . . Because our eyes are open.

Another group start off on the fact that you can go blind if light gets into your eyes (the teacher had previously warned the children not to look at the sun when they were trying the pupil investigation) and she has to redirect their attention to the original question she asked. Later she presses the children for further explanation when she says 'How did we catch it?':

R: Because you get blind.
B: When light comes in your eyes, you go to hospital.
Teacher: But when you just want to see something . . .
B: The light comes out of the eye.
A: The sun is out and the lights are on. When you turn the light on it comes in our eyes, when you turn it off, it doesn't.
M: Electricity comes into the light and it gets on. We catch some light.
Teacher: How do we catch it?
M: By our eye.

The teacher posed the question 'Do our pupils look the same all the time?' to one group of children prior to their watching the pupils of her eyes during the demonstration. One child shows quite clearly that he had noticed the phenomenon before, or at least had read about it in the book which was available in the classroom:

N: Yes.
A: Sometimes big, sometimes, small. Near the window they go smaller near the sun.

The question 'Why do you think they go smaller and bigger?' provoked interesting answers, including a sense of wonderment in the use of the word 'magic'. I suppose on reflection it is like magic: it happens all by itself, you do not appear to do anything and you cannot feel it happening! From another group it elicited the comment that the child was making a connection with a previous experience of watching her baby sister's eyes:

V: It's magic.
B: Because the light comes in, it goes smaller . . . it's magic.

A: The little bit of thing under your eye – when it's dark, dark gets into your eyes and gets it bigger. Light gets right into your eyes and it gets small.

N: When my baby sister opens her eyes, the pupils go smaller.

M: If we were in the cupboard and it was dark we couldn't read.

K: More light gets in our eyes when it's bigger.

B: It scares someone in the dark.

During discussion of the pupil in the topic book (the pupil as a window), the following exchanges occurred, showing that some are connecting the pupil with light going *into* the eye:

M: First they punched a hole in your eye then they put it in.

A: I knew it was a hole – the light gets into your eye.

A: When your eyes need only a little light they [pupils] go smaller.

B: When you go to sleep and you want to see, then you open your eyes and light comes through.

L: [having considered the pupil as a window, said with a sudden look of illumination] The light gets in!

In reflecting on the studies on pupil size (through investigation and reading in books) the teacher commented:

I learnt from this exercise the value of working in small enough groups to ensure the quiet children have their say; the value of providing occasions when assessment of understanding is through activity rather than paper-bound recording. It was also noticeable that however well structured an investigation, children may well often reach true understanding when left to explore by themselves. It was interesting too, how much better the children could relate to the factual information in a topic book, once they had experienced the phenomenon involved. Yet how many times do we as teachers attempt to introduce a topic by using books as starting points?

The drawings of sources of light provided the teacher with the opportunity to talk with children individually. When asked about the cat's eyes, C commented that 'They've got eyes and at night they make you look, in the morning you can't see the eyes properly.' When she was asked why you can't see them in the morning, she explained 'because it's too bright'. It seemed to the teacher that C was relating back to a previous conversation about the fact that fireworks can be seen better at night than during the day, because 'it's too bright in the morning'.

A conversation with D about his drawing shows the difficulty of children distinguishing a source of light from something that is bright:

Teacher: What have you drawn coming from the room light?

D: That's the light . . . it sort of . . . comes off in lines. You can see it when you switch on.

Teacher: Why did you draw the light like that? [pointing to representation of torch beam]

D: Because it come out . . . goes like that . . . and then stops.

Teacher: Does a cloud give us light?

D: Yes, they are very bright.

'This was unexpected and is probably because D is linking 'light' and 'bright' – not entirely mistakenly so. My only idea was to call his attention to clouds on a dark gloomy or rainy day when the sun was hidden and compare that to the bright sunny day when the clouds appeared white.'

Conversations with the children towards the end revealed a growing awareness of the importance of eyes for seeing and that somehow light was connected with seeing. I shall end the chapter with the teacher's own summary from her original account.

The teacher's reflections as summary

The children's responses to the different activities were as varied as their individual development. Some of the children reached their potential early on and tended to see the activities as enjoyable isolated incidents, while others with more maturity of thought took new ideas on board, tested them and then applied their new-found knowledge and skills to other situations . . . However there was no guarantee that the children interpreted the new experiences and concepts in exactly the way I had intended. 'Interpretation' is a very personal process influenced by a whole range of factors, including previous experience, knowledge and prejudice. This applies as much to children as it does to adults. Nor is this a startling revelation. Tolstoy in *War and Peace*, Volume 1, Book Two, part III encapsulates much of the spirit of what Osborne, Freyberg and Harlen have generally argued is the case for children. Count Pierre Bezukhov has been trying to put across his ideas to fellow freemasons but notes:

> At the meeting he was struck for the first time by the endless variety of men's minds, which prevents a truth from ever presenting itself identically to two persons. Even those members who seemed to be on his side understood him in their own way, with limitations and alterations he could not agree to, as what he always wanted most was to convey his thought to others just as he himself understood it.

Although arguing a point of philosophy as opposed to 'science' Tolstoy highlights the problem of interpretation.

Any development in the scientific thinking and understanding of young children has to build upon the base which already exists and make allowances for what the children bring with them. No outcome is ultimately predictable, because the individual child 'will organise their experiences into some pattern personal to themselves' (Schools Council 1972: 5).

It is for the teacher such as myself to provide the structure and opportunity for children to experience new concepts in a meaningful way, and to provide them with examples of good scientific methodology. Helping them to develop their process skills as part and parcel of the actual concepts, enables the children to explore and investigate to the best of their ability. Above all one requires endless patience because the process resembles a journey where you take five steps forward only to take three steps back.

Part 3

Part 3

9

From action to reflection

This last chapter is devoted to stepping back from the busy class-rooms to review the events that occurred within them, in light of the discussions in Chapters 1 and 2.

Knowing some science

In Chapter 2, elements of what 'knowing some science' might mean were outlined. The contribution of the teaching described in the case studies to this knowing is fairly self-evident. The children know more things than they did before, not just as information or facts from books, but as information which is understood and can be related to experiences they have had and to things that they have explored in their own environment. They have enhanced their understanding of scientific concepts. They have realized that 'in science' teachers expect them to ask questions and to give explanations; they are involved in wresting information from practical experiences by drawing and investigating; they are encouraged to look at their data and consider evidence seriously. Several of the studies relate their classroom studies to large scale phenomena (the river Thames, the Channel tunnel) and many have examples of environmental issues being illuminated by an understanding of science.

Knowing about the natural and made worlds

The children have learnt a whole range of information about the natural and made world: about the organs inside their bodies, about their heartbeat and how its rate of beating increases with exercise; about the number of bones in their bodies and that there are muscles joined to the bones; about the many different minibeasts that live almost undetected in the school grounds, about their life cycles and what they might eat; about fish having scales and how their tails move to make them go forwards; about the complex flow patterns as water runs down a channel; about the erosion of soil and mud; about the fact that rocks can absorb a considerable volume of water and that tunnels need to be lined; about the pupil of the eye changing shape in different light conditions. Perhaps the child's account at the end of Chapter 6 about what he had learnt about the Channel tunnel – where there was so much learnt that he could hardly get it all down on paper – gives an indication of just how much 'general knowledge' about science can be learnt in one of these topics.

Understanding explanation

There are many instances where the teachers asked children to make links between pieces of information, and in doing so were hunting for explanations, while at the same time introducing new concepts. The concept of the 'function' of parts of a system appeared in several of the studies: the function of the fins and tail of the fish for movement; the function of the paddle in making the boat move; the function of joints in enabling the body to have moving parts.

Hunting for explanations and links was triggered by questions asked by the teacher such as: What does this do? How does it work? What is it for? How is it made? Why is it like that? The chapters are full of questions or discussions that require links to be made, explanations to be sought. Why do you think people found it easier to distinguish the sound of the shells than any other sound? Why did the French have to have rubber tunnel linings? Why did they build the tunnel where they did? What are the factors that make the container sink? What are the factors that give a boat a large carrying capacity? Why do you think there are so many earthworms by the car park? Why did we see so many frogs in Epping Forest on our trip out? What are the ways in which rabies can be spread? Why can't we see when we turn the light out? Why can't we do a jigsaw when we shut our eyes? How does a compass work? How do you find your way underground?

Work was planned so that opportunities for making explanations were provided. In the paddle boat, the teacher deliberately gave precise instructions, with minimal choice over design, so that everyone would have a successful boat and hence have a chance of explaining how the boat worked. It would be easy for a teacher to make the construction of the boat take up so much time that there was no time for explaining.

Being familiar with scientific concepts

It is impossible to say that someone 'has' a concept that is complete, finished, polished and stable for ever. The case studies give 'windows' on emerging concepts. The list at the end of Chapter 3 gives an indication of a typical way in which a teacher might describe how far children have reached in their understanding. The list gives the concepts intrinsic to the topic with descriptions of the sort of understanding that the children were acquiring.

The means by which the teacher found out about the children's understanding as she went about the day-to-day teaching paralleled the techniques used in much of the research described in Chapter 2, i.e. listening to the children's statements and questions, looking at the products of their work, watching their interactions with tasks, noting the books they could understand. She was aware that by the end of the topic children could say far more in response to the question 'What is a wood?' than they said at the start; they would be able to give more examples of something or describe their characteristics in answer to questions like 'Tell me about insects'; or by being able to explain a phenomenon, in answer to questions like 'How do you get new plants?'

The development of concepts involves the enlargement of knowledge and often makes the knowledge less tied to one specific instance. It also often involves the ability to articulate intuitive knowledge. In the topic on the river Thames, the children ended with a far better appreciation of the concept of a 'fish'; they thought they knew what a fish looked like until they were asked to draw it; they thought they knew what a fish was, until they were asked to define it; they thought they knew how a fish moved until they looked. They ended with knowledge that they would be able to apply to a question, 'Is a shark a fish?', with a chance of answering 'Yes', whereas before the topic the automatic answer would probably have been 'No'.

In the Channel tunnel project the Year 6 group have enlarged their concept of 'rocks' by looking at several different types, by knowing that rocks have different hardnesses, different colours, different fracturing properties, different structures . . . They have altered their idea that a rock (or set of rocks as on a continent) is fixed for ever, to an awareness that rocks are being continuously recycled within the earth's crust. They might have reservations about the expression 'as solid as a rock'.

They have enlarged their concept of properties of materials in relation to materials other than rocks: the linings of the tunnel, the materials for the tunnel boring machines. They have thought again about the concept of an environment and the making of a landscape which will be a suitable habitat for certain plants and animals.

By making a model tunnel boring machine, they will have used their knowledge of electric circuits and motors and hence reinforced the ideas that they had previously.

The Year 1 group have a richer knowledge of the eye, both of its structure and its function. They have a growing awareness of what is a source of light, and that when there is no source of light it is dark.

The Year 2 group know lots of individual facts about their bodies, but are beginning to think of the body as made up of parts that 'do something'; it is the start of the recognition that the body can be thought of as a highly complex living 'machine' made up of several organs.

Asking questions

The children in the case studies asked quite a lot of scientific questions. The Year 2 class in Chapter 5 learnt how to ask questions from their ID cards, repeating the exercise with different pairs of variables (handspan and arm length, height and spine length). Just learning what questions were was an important part of the work.

The teacher in Chapter 3 (Parks, woods and wastelands) structured her teaching to work with the way people slowly grope towards the asking of questions. She recognized that encounters were important, but enhanced the chance of something coming out of the encounters by alerting children to the importance of using their senses. She had many activities which involved children in working with, or finding out, information about minibeasts (some of this was from observing the minibeasts themselves, some was from what people had written in books). She recognized that during these activities children's own questions would arise and, by having Professor Question in the classroom, had a means of collecting them for later consideration. The generation and collection of questions occurred over a period of about three weeks; the sorting of the questions took place once sufficient questions had been collected; the sorting exercise generated even more questions; the final selection of ones which could be investigated was an important activity in its own right, even before the investigations were undertaken; the undertaking of the investigations generated still more questions. The structure of her teaching had worked with the natural flow of the mental processes while at the same time enhancing what could be achieved through them.

The same teacher commented that she could judge the level of understanding by the questions which were being asked; when group A asked only very general questions, she decided that they needed more experience and knowledge of living things and of habitats. She was effectively acknowledging that the more people know about something the more they are likely to ask questions, and also that the more they know, the more they *have confidence* to ask questions.

Some of the confidence to ask questions is generated by the teacher valuing questions and the teacher modelling the asking of questions herself. Some comes from the children learning to value questions in their own right as a way into further knowledge and understanding. The latter will only come if children do indeed have success in using their questions fruitfully.

It seems important to get away from the notion that questions come bubbling out of children in a form that is easy to use and that children will automatically ask questions about all the things teachers want them to learn. The very deliberate strategies used by the teachers in the case studies to enhance the children's ability to ask well-focused questions and to know how to go about answering them should at least give pause for thought, if not challenge the notion entirely.

It would be a mistake to leave this section without acknowledging the role teachers' own knowledge plays in their willingness to entertain questioning. Research shows that teachers become more and more didactic, adopting a 'transmission' mode of teaching, the less they know about a subject. Does the willingness of the teachers in the six case studies to encourage and foster the asking of questions represent in fact a considerable knowledge of science?

Understanding experiments

The PACKS research highlighted the fact that knowing how to proceed in an investigation requires knowledge of procedures. Knowledge cannot be built up without experience, but experience alone is not sufficient. The teacher plays a significant role in her discussions with pupils about their experiences.

The case studies in Chapters 3, 4 and 8 have the most detailed accounts of teachers helping children to sort out the design of the investigations. In each case the teachers *support* the children in decision making, they do not make the decisions for them. They help the children think about all the facets of the investigation (see Rabbit's House in Chapter 4, and the earthworm study in Chapter 3). In both of these cases the teachers discussed the work sufficiently beforehand with the children for them to get started in a sensible way, but left one or two loose ends so that when the children embarked on the investigation there were still features to think about.

Teachers also have to help modify designs which would otherwise make an investigation invalid. For instance, the teacher in Chapter 8 had to help the children understand why their investigation on whether people could build a bird table with and without their eyes shut, or with and without the instructions, confused the person being tested. She had to help them test only one variable at a time instead of two.

While much of the success of the investigations lay in the teachers being able to anticipate (and support the children through) the different stages of the investigations, some resulted from their ability to identify relatively simple investigations that were appropriate and could be done within the constraints that operate in primary classrooms.

Interpreting data

Research from APU, from the studies in Durham and from the PACKS project shows that without help many learners pay little attention to evidence or perhaps need far more help than is often recognized in being able to make sense of it.

The case studies show several strategies teachers used to help children value data and to go back to the evidence they had in front of them. There is the Year 1 group in Chapter 8 having to face up to the evidence that they could not cut out circles with their eyes shut, even though they believed strongly beforehand that they could. Part of this teacher's success came from the fact that the evidence could easily be recorded so that children had something tangible to go back to and talk about. She had similarly found two simple ways to display the eye colour of all the children, so that it was possible to see the proportion of different colour eyes in the class.

The teacher of the Year 4 class in Chapter 7, in the river Thames topic, insisted that the children kept going back to the object or phenomenon under observation and drawing and writing about what they *saw*, not what they *knew*. Her insistence on this valuing of evidence improved the quality of observation both in the cases of the fish and prawn and the later work on the paddle boat and water flow in the channel.

The teacher of the Years 1 and 2 class who helped the children examine the data from Rabbit's House used a well-tried technique for looking at data, i.e. she asked the children merely to describe it first. Often interpretation starts too early, before people have had a good look at what is there. Just as the teacher in Chapter 6 asked the children to look at the structure and the movement of fish, before she linked structure and movement, so having a good look at the data should precede interpretation and explanation. The questions used to help children describe the data in Rabbit's House were: 'Which one has more ticks than crosses?'

'Which has more crosses than ticks?' 'Where are they the same?' 'What else do you notice?' 'Which ones did children try the most?' She often followed her questions with another, 'How do you know?', requiring more detailed description of the evidence. She used comparison, 'Did everyone find that?', and made the children search the other recording sheets to see if there were similar patterns there.

Only when the data had been described did she seek explanations: 'Why do you think children tried that one the most?' 'Which was the most difficult to identify?' 'How do you know?' 'Why do you think that was so?' 'Did everyone find that?' 'Which was the easiest?' The conclusions drawn were tentative: 'Christopher thought . . .'

The children in the Year 2 class trying to answer the questions from their ID cards had been taught a simple technique for exploring data: they put the information in numerical order, not by rearranging it physically on the table, but by marking the order with 1, 2, 3, 4, etc. against the measurements.

Valid conclusions can of course only be drawn from evidence if the evidence itself is valid. Poor design of investigations generates useless evidence; if children are to value the evidence, they must value the design. The evidence can also be spoiled if the necessary technical know-how and practical skills are not there to execute the investigation well.

Having technical know-how

The case studies give examples of the children learning or practising a range of technical tasks which will increase their manipulative skills and their general technical competence: handling small animals without damaging them; using hand lenses; measuring out the area to be used for the earthworm search; developing the fine control needed for using dropping pipettes to add drops of ink to the water flowing down the channel; using a cutting knife to cut the corroflute accurately, pressing pins vertically through the paper on to the corroflute in order to transfer the plan from paper to plastic; using the weighing scales for the chalk and measuring cylinders for estimating the volume of water absorbed; using scissors for the many investigations in 'Seeing and light'.

Linking science and everyday occurrences

Science in primary schools has the advantage that it is often set within an integrated topic, whereby the science is automatically embedded within a context which is wider than the science itself and which has strong elements of the 'everyday' about it: the parks and woodlands, the river Thames, the Channel tunnel, the human body . . .

Appreciating the nature of science

The Pine class scientist embodies a lot of the nature of science. It is probably worth going back to the picture on page 82 and noting the many aspects of science which are incorporated in this image.

It is hard to tell what picture of science is building up in these children's minds even though most facets of 'knowing some science' are present in all the case studies. I suspect, however, that what enables these teachers to take children on a journey which does justice to the children and the subject is that they have an appreciation of the nature of science themselves and are aware of the different elements. They will vary in their knowledge of specific facts and explanations, and the extent to which their knowledge of the nature of science is articulated.

Appreciating the cultural significance of science

It is a tall order for young children to recognize the cultural significance of science; the groundwork is, nevertheless, being laid at this stage. We can note that the Year 6 class became fully involved in understanding the legal controls necessary for preventing animals coming through the tunnel, and that they became aware that just because it is possible to do something (in this case build the tunnel) then it is not necessarily the right thing to do.

Construction and reconstruction of knowledge as a means of knowing

In reviewing the case studies in the light of the discussion of 'knowing some science' I have also discussed many of the strategies that teachers used to organize, plan and manage the learning, and in so doing have returned to the themes in Chapter 1. There is, however, one theme, the children as 'meaning makers' in the classroom, that I want to separate out for special mention, before ending with some of the features that were important to the six teachers and a final thought about creativity.

Much of the new-found understanding of facts, concepts and explanations is inextricably linked to the practical experiences that teachers provide, combined with the mental processing *and reprocessing* of ideas through talking, writing, reading, drawing and model making.

The case studies are full of examples of the deliberate use of the fact that writing, drawing, or talking about a subject being learnt is an intrinsic part of that learning. The preparation of the class book of Rabbit's House required the children to reflect on what they had learnt, systematize it, and in doing so enabled them to learn it better. When the class settled to writing the questionnaire about people's attitudes to the Channel tunnel, they were forced to think quite deeply about what it was they wanted to know. The use of 'jigsawing' in the organization of the book research on boats in the case study on the river Thames required the children not only to find out information from books, but to reconstruct it for another audience. In the same topic, children not only wrote their own observations of the flow of water in the channel, and in doing so, clarified their own understanding, they also had to reconstruct their knowledge in combining it with that of other children to produce their shared writing. It is no wonder that the teachers place such a high value on children's ability to communicate in as many ways as possible; because in the process of communicating, new understandings are formed. Language was high on the agenda for them all. I have included in the references two books by Karen Gallas (1994, 1995) in which she explores the role of language and communication in the learning of science.

Many of the techniques which the teachers used in helping children make sense of information from secondary sources can be found elaborated in books such as those by Mallett (1992) and Neate (1992).

Features important to the six teachers

In his article about what knowledge teachers need for subject teaching, McDiarmid Williamson and colleagues (1987: 194) wrote:

'Connecting pupils with subject matter entails weaving together ideas about how people learn and knowledge about particular pupils with a thorough understanding of the subject in ways that respect the integrity of each.'

In the conversations with the six teachers whose case studies appear in Chapters 3 to 8, each teacher invariably selected, without prompting, events that were of particular significance. I hope that in writing the case studies I have adequately indicated them. They all centred on 'connecting the pupil . . .' and knowing that a connection had been made. Here are just a few: Professor Sense and Professor Question in Chapter 3; the joy of realizing that patterns in data emerge 'as you go along' if you use the modified table in Rabbit's House; the realization that it is possible to investigate yourself in Chapter 6; the problem of the tunnel to the swimming pool in Chapter 7 helping children understand the issues involved in tunnel building; the amazement and distress of children in Chapter 8 when they found that they could not cut out circles with their eyes closed, but the laughter and understanding that accompanied the later investigations.

Teachers' actions were also selected for special mention, such as the teacher in Chapter 3 consciously holding back on answering questions to give children space to come up with their own ideas; the teacher in Chapter 4 leaving 'a loose end' in the design of a table so she could raise the question of modification and improvement; the teacher in Chapter 7 emphasizing the constant reviewing of learning which she did with the whole class, and the way she was consciously acting as a role model on how to review learning; the teacher in Chapter 8 taking part in the investigations to reduce the anxiety of children 'failing' in investigations.

What came through all their conversations was an intrinsic interest in the learning process; in what was learnt; in how they as teachers knew what was learnt; in understanding the process of learning itself; and in their own role in this process.

Mary Jane Drummond wrote in her book, *Assessing Children's Learning* (1994: 10): 'It is children's learning that must be the subject of teachers' most energetic care and attention – not their lesson plans, or their schemes of work, or their rich and stimulating provision – but the learning that results from everything they do (and do not do) in schools and classrooms.'

On the same page she wrote: 'The process of assessing children's learning – by looking closely at it and striving to understand it

– is the only certain safeguard against children's failure, the only certain guarantee of children's progress and development.'

The case studies provide examples of what this looks like in practice and how such a focus on children's learning can be an intrinsic part of science teaching in primary classrooms. It is no coincidence that Esmé Glauert (the teacher of Rabbit's House) has just published a book herself to help teachers track children's significant achievement in science (Glauert 1996).

Creativity

I suspect that it is the focus on learning that is the main driving force behind the creativity. In striving to ensure that every child learns and makes connections with the essential elements of science, these teachers have created a wide range of strategies and activities for their classrooms.

They have learnt ways of talking about science appropriately with children of different ages; and more importantly they have been able to get the children themselves talking seriously about science. They have also been able to provide sufficiently tight frameworks in terms of resources, classroom organization and time management, that they have been free to be creative.

They have written and resourced their draft 'plays' in their plans, but the final performance is always different, because teaching provides both the opportunity and the necessity to be creative.

Bibliography

Aardema, V. (1978) *Who's in Rabbit's House?* London: Bodley Head.

Baird, M. and J. (1994) Science: Little Red Riding Hood, *Guardian Education Supplement*, 6 December.

Carré, C. G. and Carter, D. S. G. (1993) Primary teachers' self perceptions concerning implementation of the national curriculum for science in the UK – revisited, *International Journal of Science Education*, 15(4): 457–70.

Department for Education [DFE] (1995) *National Curriculum: Science.* London: HMSO.

Department of Education and Science [DES] (1989) *National Assessment. The APU Science Approach.* London: HMSO.

Driver, R., Squires, A., Rushworth, P. and Wood-Robinson, V. (1994) *Making Sense of Secondary Science: Research into Children's Ideas.* London: Routledge.

Driver, R., Tiberghien, A. and Guesne, E. (1985) *Children's Ideas in Science.* Milton Keynes: Open University Press.

Drummond, M. J. (1994) *Assessing Children's Learning.* London: David Fulton.

Elstgeest, J. (1985a) Encounter, interaction, dialogue, in W. Harlen (ed.) *Primary Science – Taking the Plunge.* London: Heinemann Educational Books.

Elstgeest, J. (1985b) The right question at the right time, in W. Harlen, *Primary Science – Taking the Plunge*. London: Heinemann Educational Books.

Elstgeest, J. (1992) Engaging children in active science in the primary school, in W. Harlen and J. Elstgeest, *Unesco Sourcebook for Science in the Primary School*. Paris: UNESCO Publishing.

Feasey, R. and Thomas, L. (1993) *Effective Questioning in Science*. Durham: University of Durham School of Education.

Foulds, K., Gott, R. and Feasey, R. (1992) *Investigative Work in Science. A Report by the Exploration of Science Team to the National Curriculum Council*. Durham: University of Durham.

Frost, J., Macaskill, C. and Cuthbertson, A. (1993) Practical activities and fair tests: reflections from the Aquatech Project, *Primary Science Review*. 26: 14.

Gallas, K. (1994) *The Languages of Learning: How Children Talk, Write, Dance, Draw and Sing their Understanding of the World*. New York: Teachers College Press.

Gallas, K. (1995) *Taking their Way into Science: Hearing Children's Questions and Theories: Responding with Curricula*. New York: Teachers College Press.

Glauert, E. (1996) *Tracking Significant Achievement in Primary Science*. London: Hodder & Stoughton.

Goldsworthy, A. and Feasey, R. (1994) *Making Sense of Primary Science Investigations*. Hatfield: ASE.

Grimwade, K. (1987) *Discover Physical Geography*. London: Hodder & Stoughton.

Harlen, W. (1995) *Teaching and Learning Primary Science*, 3rd edn. London: Paul Chapman Publishing.

Harlen, W., Holdroyd, C. and Byrne, M. (1995) *Confidence and Understanding in Teaching Science and Technology in Primary Schools*. Edinburgh: Scottish Council for Research in Education.

Jelly, S. (1985) Helping children raise questions – and answering them, in W. Harlen (ed.) *Primary Science – Taking the Plunge*. London: Heinemann Educational Books.

Kinder, K. and Harland, J. (1991) *The Impact of INSET: the Case of Primary Science*. Slough: NFER.

Mallett, M. (1992) *Making Facts Matter. Reading Non-fiction 5–11*. London: Hodder and Stoughton.

McDiarmid Williamson, G., Loewenberg Ball, D. and Anderson, C. W. (1987) Why staying one chapter ahead doesn't really work: subject specific pedagogy, in M. C. Reynolds (ed.) *Knowledge Base for the Beginning Teacher*. Oxford: Pergamon Press.

Neate, B. (1992) *Finding out about Finding out: a Practical Guide to Children's Information Books*. London: Hodder and Stoughton.

Nussbaum, G. (1985) The earth as a cosmic body, in R. Driver, A. Tiberghien and E. Guesne, *Children's Ideas in Science*. Milton Keynes: Open University Press.

Office for Standards in Education [OFSTED] (1995) *Science. A Review of Inspection Findings 1993/4*. London: HMSO.

Ollerenshaw, C. and Ritchie, R. (1993) *Primary Science – Making it Work*. London: David Fulton.

Osborne, R. and Freyberg, P. (1985) *Learning in Science*. Auckland, New Zealand: Heinemann.

Reasoner, C. (1995) *Who's Hatching?* New York: Golden Books.

Schools Council (1972) *With Objectives in Mind, Guide to Science 5–13*. London: Schools Council in conjunction with Macdonald Education.

Shulman, L. S. (1986) Those who understand: knowledge growth in teaching, *Educational Researcher*, 15(2): 4–14.

Summers, M. and Kruger, C. (1992) Research into English primary school teachers' understanding of the concept energy, in L. Newton (ed.) *Primary Science: the Challenge of the 1990s*. Clevedon: Multilingual Matters.

Wragg, E. (1994) Teachers' subject knowledge, in A. Pollard and J. Bourne *Teaching and Learning in the Primary School*. Buckingham: Open University Press.

Wragg, E., Bennett, S. and Carré, C. (1989) Primary teachers and the National Curriculum, *Research Papers in Education*, 4(3): 17–45.

Research Projects in Science Education

Assessment of Performance Unit [APU]: 'Science Reports for Teachers' series. Hatfield: ASE.

Black, P. (1990) APU Science – the past and the future, *School Science Review*, 72(258): 13–28.

Harlen, W. (1983) No. 1 *Science at Age 11*

Harlen, W. (1986) No. 8 *Planning Investigations at Age 11*

Harlen, W., Palacio, D. and Russell, T. (1984) No. 2 *Science Assessment Framework: Age 11*

Russell, T., Black, P., Harlen, W., Johnson, S. and Palacio, D. (1988) *Science at Age 11. A Review of APU Survey Findings 1980–1984*. London: HMSO.

Walford, G., Harlen, W. and Scholfield, B. (1985) No. 6 *Practical Testing at 11, 13 and 15*

Children's Learning in Science [CLIS] **Project**

CLIS (1992) Progression in Understanding of Ecological Concepts by Pupils Age 5 to 16. Leeds: University of Leeds.

See references to Driver *et al.* (1985, 1994) and Osborne and Freyberg (1985) above for extensive bibliographies not only to the CLIS Project at Leeds but to related research worldwide. Most of the CLIS titles refer to the secondary age range, but the techniques have been applied to the primary age range and influenced particularly the way in which the SPACE project was carried out.

Procedural and Conceptual Knowledge in Science [PACKS]
Duggan, S., Gott, R., Lubben, F., Millar, R. (1994) Evidence in science, in M. Hughes, *Teaching and Learning in Changing Times*. Oxford: Blackwell.
Gott, R., Duggan, S., Millar, R. and Lubben, F. (1994) 'Evidence – a black hole in the teaching of science'. Paper presented to the British Association for the Advancement of Science, September.
Millar, R., Lubben, F., Gott, R. and Duggan, S. (1994) Investigating in the school science laboratory: conceptual and procedural knowledge and their influence on performance, Special issue of *Research Papers in Education*, June 1994.

Science Process and Concept Exploration [SPACE] **Project**
Osborne, J., Black, P., Smith, M. and Meadows, J. (1990) *Electricity*
Osborne, J., Black, P., Smith, M. and Meadows, J. (1990) *Light*
Osborne, J., Wadsworth, P. and Black, P. (1992) *Processes of Life*
Russell, T., Bell, D., Longdean, K. and McGuigan, L. (1993) *Rocks, Soil and Weather*
Russell, T., Longdean, K. and McGuigan, L. (1991) *Materials*
Russell, T. and Watt, D. (1990a) *Evaporation and Condensation*
Russell, T. and Watt, D. (1990b) *Growth*
Watt, D. and Russell, T. (1990) *Sound*

Science Teacher Action Research [STAR] **Project** 'Assessing Science in the Primary Classroom' series. London: Paul Chapman.
Cavendish, S., Galton, M., Hargreaves, L. and Harlen, W. (1990) *Observing Activities*
Russell, T. and Harlen, W. (1990) *Practical Tasks*
Schilling, M., Hargreaves, L., Harlen, W. and Russell, T. (1990) *Written Tasks*

Index

EARLY EXPLORATIONS IN SCIENCE

Jane Johnston

The introduction of the National Curriculum in science at Key Stage 1 has highlighted the need for a close look at teaching and learning in early years science. Children are immersed in science through their everyday experiences and these early science experiences will shape their future development.

This book explores issues such as the range, nature and importance of pre-school and Key Stage 1 science experiences. It considers the development of scientific skills, conceptual understanding and attitudes in young children, through observation, exploration and creative activities. Throughout there is an attempt to engage the reader in thoughtful consideration of their role in early scientific development and of the important role played by parents and children themselves. The book will be invaluable reading for all trainee and practising primary school teachers.

This book:

- provides several examples of stimulating and creative classroom activities;
- is accessibly written to support teachers and build confidence in teaching primary science;
- is firmly grounded in good early years practice.

Contents
Pre-school science experiences – The importance of exploration in the development of early years science knowledge and skills – Seeking creativity in science activities – Developing positive attitudes in science – Developing the teacher's role – References – Index.

184pp   0 335 19540 7 (Paperback)   0 335 19541 5 (Hardback)

DIFFERENTIATED PRIMARY SCIENCE
Anne Qualter

- What is differentiation?
- How can it be put into practice in primary science lessons?
- Is it *really* possible to provide differentiated learning activities for a class of thirty or more primary children?

Taking a refreshingly pragmatic approach, Anne Qualter addresses these challenging issues in this book. Drawing on her own experience as a classroom teacher combined with research undertaken in a wide range of primary classrooms, the author shows that genuinely differentiated primary science *is* achievable. Using several classroom examples, she argues that differentiation is not simply about categorizing children as more or less able but involves the teacher in complex decisions which take account of the child's understanding and capabilities, their cultural background, gender, linguistic capabilities, interests and a variety of other factors.

The book will be invaluable reading for both trainee and practising primary school teachers.

Contents
The place of differentiation in primary science – What do we mean by ability in science? – Finding starting points – Factors influencing children's science – Developing models for differentiated learning – The process of differentiation – Bibliography – Index.

208pp   0 335 19575 X (Paperback)   0 335 19576 8 (Hardback)

ORGANIZING FOR LEARNING IN THE PRIMARY CLASSROOM
A BALANCED APPROACH TO CLASSROOM MANAGEMENT

Janet R. Moyles

What is it that underlies classroom organization, routines, rules, structures and daily occurrences? What are the prime objectives and what influences the decisions of teachers and children? What is it useful for teachers to consider when contemplating the issues of classroom management and organization? What do different practices have to offer?

Organizing for Learning in the Primary Classroom explores the whole range of influences and values which underpin *why* teachers do *what* they do in the classroom context and what these mean to children and others. Janet Moyles examines teaching and learning styles, children's independence and autonomy, coping with children's differences, the physical classroom context and resources, time management and ways of involving others in the day-to-day organization. Practical suggestions are given for considering both the functional and aesthetic aspects of the classroom context. Opportunities are provided for teachers to reflect on their own organization and also consider innovative and flexible ways forward to deal with new and ever increasing demands on their time and sanity!

> This book is to be highly recommended for all primary school teachers . . . (*Management in Education*)

> . . . indispensable to courses in initial teacher education and to providers of inset. (*Child Education*)

> Janet Moyles brings her long experience of the primary school to *Organizing for Learning in the Primary Classroom* . . . I particularly like the attention she gives to the physical environment, giving lots of advice about arrangements of furniture and the role of the teacher's desk . . . (*Times Educational Supplement*)

Contents
Introduction: Polarizations and balance – Teachers and teaching: beliefs and values – The learning environment: organizing the classroom context – The children and their learning needs: balancing individual and whole class approaches – Grouping children for teaching and learning: providing equal opportunities and promoting appropriate behaviour – Time for teaching and learning – Deploying adult help effectively in the classroom: delegation and responsibility – Evaluating classroom organization and management – Conclusion: the primary classroom, a place and a time – References – Index.

208pp   0 335 15659 2 (Paperback)   0 335 15660 6 (Hardback)